OUT OF ORDER

OUT OF ORDER

More Irregular Essays from
PUBLIC RADIO

DAVID BOUCHIER

LUMINARE PRESS
WWW.LUMINAREPRESS.COM

Out of Order: More Irregular Essays from Public Radio
Copyright © 2021 by David Bouchier

All rights reserved. This book or any portion thereof may not be reproduced or used in any manner whatsoever without the express written permission of the publisher, except for the use of brief quotations in a book review.

Printed in the United States of America

Luminare Press
442 Charnelton St.
Eugene, OR 97401
www.luminarepress.com

LCCN: 2021906317
ISBN: 978-1-64388-650-3

For Diane

As always

Also by David Bouchier:

Journal of the Eightieth Year

Dark Matters

An Unexpected Life

Out of Thin Air

Lucky Man

Peripheral Vision

A Few Well Chosen Words

Not Quite a Stranger

The Song of Suburbia

The Cats and the Water Bottles

Writer at Work

The Accidental Immigrant

Radical Citizenship

The Feminist Challenge

Idealism and Revolution

CONTENTS

PART ONE:
THE HUMAN COMEDY

The Summer of Love 7

A Wilderness of Cars. 10

The Revenge of Paper 13

Fear of Physics. 16

Magical Thinking 19

Martin Luther Drains the Swamp 22

Family Secrets 24

The Creative Hut. 26

Taking the Long View 29

You Can Bet On It 32

A New Royal Family 35

Right on Schedule 38

Here Goes Nothing 41

Lost in Space 44

No Complaints 47

The World Really Is a Stage 50

Slow News 53

Little Brother. 56

Complicated 58

Worth a Thousand Words? 61

Polyglot 64

The Makeover 67

The Pleasure of Rituals 70
There's a Hole in My Bucket List. 72
Ancestor Worship 75
Eyes Down 79
Intelligence Test 82
The Annual New Start 85
Small Worlds 87
Strange Encounters......................... 89
Time after Time 92
The Valentine Contract....................... 94
Please Don't Give Me the Facts................ 97
Lost in Translation 100
Please Wait............................... 103
The Kindness of Strangers 106
The Image 109
Real Work................................ 112
Stormy Weather........................... 114
Under the Influence 117
The Sounds of Silence...................... 120
Good Advice.............................. 123
Yesterday's News 126
Hunting and Gathering 129
A Short Walk in the Woods.................. 132
Everybody on Stage........................ 135
My Little Shop 138
Self-esteem for All 140

The Virus That Would Not Go Away.............143
Quarantine Memories 146
The Literary Hermit.........................149
Saving the Planet...........................152
A Symbolic Moment..........................155
Build We Must..............................158
Kindness to Animals Week...................161
Bored in the USA...........................164
Tough Guys.................................167
Travel Interrupted 170
Walls and Masks 172
The End of Education? 175
Bloomsday Unmasked........................178
Beauty and the Beast 181
Walking Alone 185
On the Beach 188
Prophets of Doom 192
A Quiet War 195
Life on Wheels.............................198
The Triumph of Parkinson 201
Professors in the Cloud......................205
The Rugged Individualist....................208
The Loneliness of the Long-Distance Consumer . 211
Pumping Irony..............................214
College on Hold............................217
What Would Victory Look Like?................220

No Respect 223
The Last Frontier. 226
A Safe Place. 230
Sitting Out the Pandemic 234
The Unanswered Question 237
Happy Winter Solstice. 240
Organizing the Future 244
Taking the Short View. 247
Help Is on the Way. 249
Goodbye to All That 252

PART TWO:
A TOXIC ELECTION SEASON

American Politics after 2016. 257
A Little History 261
Plato at the Polling Booth 266
A Modest Proposal 271
In the Footsteps of Zeus 274
The Problem of "Leadership". 277
Rough Justice. 280
The Survival of the Fittest 283
Do You Believe in Magic? 287
Vote with Your Head 290
It's All About the Money 293
The Only Thing That Might Work 295

PREFACE

My favorite philosopher David Hume turned to writing essays after working for years on long and difficult books that few readers could understand. He wrote that he considered himself "An ambassador from the world of learning to that of conversation." It's a high ambition, but I like to think that a radio essays is a conversation, or at least one side of a conversation to which every listener can respond in his or her own way. Public Radio is one of the last places on the airwaves where you can hear essays read by their authors. They are necessarily ephemeral, and usually vanish as soon as they are aired although they may have a tenuous afterlife on station web pages or as podcasts. What is the excuse for saving them in print, apart from simple vanity? Vanity is a big part of it, of course, but a writer must have some faith in his own ideas, and I would make a stronger argument. Many of these essays begin with a trivial observation of the human comedy. This is where most of us live, down among the trivia rather than in some exalted intellectual bubble. That's real life, like it or not, and real life, in all its charming confusion, is the proper subject for an essayist's curiosity. So, in this collection, I have set out to preserve some of my weekly commentaries, broadcast on National Public Radio Stations WSHU and WSUF between 2017 and the first weeks of 2021, right after the chaotic Presidential election. I would like to claim that I am saving these observations for posterity but, so far, posterity has made no such request.

Twenty-nine years have passed since I began broadcasting short essays on public radio. When I started in 1992 I was a naïve new immigrant to the United States and found everything fascinating and amusing. This fascination has not changed, although America has changed enormously. In 1992 George H. W. Bush was president until defeated by Bill Clinton in November. Boris Yeltsin ruled precariously in Russia, and Disney opened a theme park in France. There was enough material in a single year for a lifetime of commentary. Indeed, there never has been any shortage of subjects to write about. The nineties were fairly crazy, but the 2000s so far have been made to order for a writer with a sense of the ridiculous.

I have sometimes been accused of committing humor, but all I ever do is record the facts. The most obvious fact of all is that things are never what they seem, and that there is a yawning gap between life as it is and life as we imagine it should be. As Voltaire observed long ago the world is obviously absurd, but we try to make sense of it anyway. This doomed effort to make sense out of nonsense is a gift to the writer, whose job is to pull back the curtain like the little dog Toto in the Wizard of Oz, to reveal the crude machinery behind the illusion. I can't pretend to compete with the great curtain-pullers of history like Toto himself, or indeed Voltaire, but it is a goal to aim at.

The election of 2016 threatened to destroy satire entirely by shifting the boundaries of reality several steps in the direction of absurdity. It seemed like a bad dream at first, but soon it came into focus as a moment of painful self-recognition. Every observer since Ben Franklin has pointed out that the United States is really two (or more) nations with two (or more) cultures. But, since the Civil War, a thin blanket of tolerance and conformity had shielded the fact from most of us. In 2016 the Pandora's Box of racism and tribalism was brutally thrown open, leaving the country at the mercy of a rabble-rousing bankrupt real estate operator, serial sex offender, and reality TV star with the vocabulary of an eight year old and a severe case of narcissistic personality disorder. It seems that this was the best leader that two hundred and sixty million Americans could choose. Who could have made this up?

Just to make things more interesting, while an ugly and corrupt election campaign was gearing up in 2020, COVID-19 arrived turning the lives of millions upside down, and shattering the economy and social life. Most politicians, notably the President, paid no attention. They were, as always, entirely obsessed by the thought of the next election. This convergence of catastrophes made it hard to keep any sense of humor, but we did our best.

Some of the essays in this book are a personal journal of the plague year. The parallel political plague was no less deadly, but I have separated political commentaries into a separate section at the end of the book. This makes them easier to ignore, and I expect that many readers will appreciate my thoughtfulness in doing this.

The COVID-19 epidemic was a death sentence for some, an economic catastrophe for many, and a minor annoyance for me. When the virus arrived I was already old enough to have no long-term expectations, and living on an adequate pension in a comfortable detached house with a garden, in a quiet suburb, with a loving wife. I have been very lucky so far, although anything can happen. Trapped at home, I have amused myself by collecting these essays, which I hope will add a little ironic spice to our memories of American life during these three extraordinary years.

David Bouchier
Stony Brook, New York 2021

PART ONE

THE HUMAN COMEDY

The Summer of Love

Fifty years ago I lived for a while in California, and spent as much time as possible hanging around in San Francisco. This was not because of any special devotion to picturesque cable cars or overpriced fish restaurants. At that time San Francisco was ground zero for the Hippie phenomenon. Young people had flocked there from all over America and the world to create what sociologists called a "Counter Culture," and 1967 was the high point of the Counter Culture. They called it the Summer of Love. What could be more counter to our regular culture than love?

My interest was purely professional. I was already too old and cyncical to be accepted as a Hippie. The slogan of the times was "Don't trust anyone over thirty," and I was just at that untrustworthy crossroads. My hair and beard were not long enough, my taste in music was all wrong, and my drugs of choice were more conventional and more legal than theirs.

But I envied the young rebels of the Counter Culture, and hoped they would make an impact on a country that was being roiled by the Vietnam war and the aftermath of the Civil Rights Movement. In fact I was pursuing a personal research project designed to nswer that very question: could a large group of non-violent people driven by passionate ideals actually change a whole culure? It was a naïve question, and I'll save you the suspense: the answer was no.

I liked the Hippies I met, and spent time in hot tubs with them. They were gentle and humorous, mellowed by a huge consumption of marijuana, and they meant well. Their ideology, if you can call it that, was deeply un-American. They despised money and material possessions, and thought that libertarianism meant freedom to live as you liked ("Do Your Own Thing") rather than freedom to make unlimited profits through deregulation. They were doomed from the start. What kind of political program is it to say: "We should love one another." Gerry Falwell would be horrified by such a notion.

I like the idea of love, in fact I'm all in favor of it. But a whole summer of love demanded too much of human nature. The entire wistful movement dissolved into bad drug experiences, crime, and conflict with the police over petty issues like housing conditions and public nudity. On October 6th in 1967 a mock funeral for "The Hippie" was held in the Haight-Ashbury district, and that was almost the end of it.

The fiftieth anniversary of the Summer of Love has not brought much love with it. Perhaps we should try again, but on a more modest scale. The French have a National Day of Kindness once a year. Local newspapers run surveys to identify people in the area who are known for their kindness to others, and publish their names and their stories. It is a very positive and appealing campaign, and it would be nice to see more like it. But kindness is no more fashionable than love these days. Too many things conspire to make us wary of it as a form of weakness: sports, war, videogames, business, and of course, politics.

So I fear that a even whole Day of Kindness might be too much for us. Perhaps next year we could manage an afternoon of tolerance. Would that be too much to ask?

First broadcast: September 25, 2017

A Wilderness of Cars

The driver's side window of my car stuck in the open position during a rainstorm, so I drove rather damply to my usual mechanic. He inhabits a workshop in one of those areas where automotive businesses cluster, rather the way doctors' offices cluster around a hospital. It is reassuring, in a way. If one practitioner can't fix your problem, the one on the next block probably can.

My mechanic, who has kept my old car alive for years, has staked out his territory alongside a stretch of highway on which sick and broken vehicles seem to be the main and only business. While I waited I took a damp walk in the surrounding area. Each automotive establishment flowed into the next—general repair mechanics, the appropriately named body shops, tire shops, brake specialists, rapid oil change wizards, wholesalers of spare parts, and even a couple of used car dealers selling the wrecks that had been patched up by all the rest.

It was a wilderness of battered and broken cars, and it set me thinking about how we came to depend on them so much, and the price we pay for it. Here in the suburbs, many of us can scarcely even buy a loaf of bread without getting into a car. They are as essential as fresh air, not that we have much of that alongside our busy highways.

Every repair shop seemed to have a dozen or more vehicles parked outside, most of them quite new. Like mine they had all failed in some small but important way. I can remember when car engines sometimes blew up or wheels fell off. This rarely happens now. It's the small stuff that brings the big bills and my mechanic confided that much of it is not mechanical at all, but electronic. In other words the car's computer has failed. A car used to be four wheels and an engine. Why on earth should it need a computer?

Another lesson came from the body shops. A stroll through half a dozen fields of expensively smashed vehicles should be a compulsory part of every driver's education. It teaches, first of all, that the cars we trust so much are appallingly flimsy tin cans on wheels. Here you see them ripped apart in every possible way, crumpled, flattened, and reduced to unrecognizable heaps of metal. I don't know whether body shop owners are exceptionally careful drivers, but they certainly should be. Their work is a kind of daily *memento mori*.

This automotive carnage testifies to a lamentable lack of driving skills. It makes the idea of self-driving cars almost appealing. With computers at the wheel we are assured that no errors of judgement would be possible and accident rates should drop to zero. What worries me is the intermediate period, when half the cars will be guided by infallible computers, just like the one you have at home, and the other half will still be driven by the kinds of lunatics whose wreckage fills the body shops. Who will sort out the battles over legal liability? Who will pay the insurance? You already have to post a three million dollar bond to let one of these autonomous cars loose on the highways in Nevada, and there's almost no traffic in Nevada. Imagine what it would cost in New York. Who will cover the enormous repair bills? There's no Affordable Car Act. but we're going to need one before we all get grounded forever.

First broadcast: October 16, 2017

The Revenge of Paper

A few days before school started here on Long Island I went to a big office supply store in search of something old-fashioned, like filing folders or yellow pads. Dozens of eager young scholars and their teachers were there before me, stocking up for that long-awaited back-to school moment. I hoped and assumed that this mass of eager shoppers would be crowding the aisles of computers and electronic gadgets, because I had heard that nothing educational happens offline or offscreen these days. But no, they were interested only in paper, and all the charming products that accompany paper—pens and pencils, crayons, glue sticks, and folders in many colors.

One studious young man, about eight years old, reminded me of my much younger self. Back in the primitive times, when paper ruled the world, the stationery store was one of my favorite browsing places. The seemingly infinite variety of pens and inks, notebooks in different sizes, with different bindings, and pages ruled wide or narrow, had a tactile quality and an edifying smell that appealed to me, the way paints, brushes and canvases must appeal to a young artist. It seemed that anything was possible, given the right combination of paper, pen, and ink. The whole history of the world and all our best myths and stories have been created out of such simple materials. Shakespeare had nothing but pen and ink, and managed quite well with them.

So, as a child, I haunted the little stationery store in our local high street, no doubt to the anoyance of the owner. But I was amazed to see a young man of the twenty-first century doing much the same thing here and now. He picked over the hundreds of pens like a connoisseur assessing a display of fine miniatures. He opened the notebooks one by one, riffling through the blank pages and frowning in concentration. Clearly he considered that putting pen to paper was a serious business, and of course he was right. In spite of all the efforts of the electronic industrial complex, paper still rules the world. Global paper production is way up, and the average American consumes five hundred pounds per year, about the weight of a large dumpster. Not all of this is school related, of course. A lot of it is junk mail, and most of the rest is accounted for by the Government Printing Office in Washington DC that produces tens of thousands of copies of reports, bills, and regulations for the federal bureaucracy, all destined for the shredder.

But even so the schools seem to be falling behind the times. What happened to the educational revolution? No modern child should have to come home at the end of the school day with hands and clothes covered in ink, the way we used to do. But it seems that, for once, I am wrong. Paper and writing are still part of the school experience. Some of the childen leaving the office store were so loaded down with paper products that it was hard to see how they would find time to surf the internet or check their twitter accounts in the classroom.

It may be that teachers of a certain age grew up with paper and print, and simply feel more comfortable with these old-fashioned materials. Or perhaps all of us, young and old, are uneasily aware of the fragility of the electronic universe, already deeply compromised by global hackers and cyber-criminals. Nothing is safe, not even in the famous "cloud" which is nothing but another bunch of computers somewhere in Arizona. The cloud may blow away one day, leaving nothing but blue skies and blank screens. Then we will urgently need a nice notebook, and a pen, and some colored folders, and perhaps a glue stick too. It's always best to be prepared.

First broadcast: September 9, 2017

Fear of Physics

My ignorance about science is virtually complete. We were given only a tiny amount of science education at school: some simplified physics and a little more or less unintelligible chemistry—literally unintelligible because it was taught by a Scotsman whose accent none of us could understand. I never learned anything more.

This scientific illiteracy has troubled me ever since. The more our world is built on and by science, the less I seem to understand about it. So recently I decided to make an effort and enrolled in a course at the university that was specifically designed to enlighten backward senior citizens like me. It was on quantum mechanics. I should have chosen something easier, like knitting. Quantum theory, for a scientific beginner, is like trying to learn orchestral conducting without first learning to read music. The first two class sessions were deeply confusing, but also intriguing. I have always lived in a Newtonian world where apples fall on your head for perfectly straightforward reasons, and the speed of light is measured by how long it takes to get to the light switch. But this was, in every sense, a different universe. Most of us can cope with a graph, a bar chart, or a bar bill, but show us (for example) a simple equation demonstratiing the Lorentz Transformation and the brain freezes. It's like confronting a restaurant menu in a foreign language. We would rather just settle for a cheese sandwich.

But my curiousity was piqued, and I might have continued with my scientific education until I had become another Einstein. What profound answers to the secrets of the universe I could have come up with if only I knew what the questions were. But an unforunate conflict of schedules cut my scientific education short before it had really started. For the first time in my life I became a college dropout long before the secrets of the universe had been revealed to me. On the other hand there was a sense of guilty relief. The full depths of my ignorance would not be tested.

We all have our limitations. Dr. Lawrence J. Peter named the problem in 1969 when he coined the phrase "Level of incompetence." It's a normal process. All of us reach our level of incompetence in various things and abandon them one after another. I have given up on many things: in my lifetime, the classical guitar, French grammar, and James Joyce's *Ulysses* among others. We succeed at some things and fail at others.

But giving up on science—on the whole *idea* of science—almost amounts to giving up on rational thought. That's why the anti-scienctific mood in Washington is so disturbing. It's not just fear of physics but fear of all the sciences, especially the ones that bring unwelcome news. Scientific answers are out. Emotionally satisfying and profitable answers are in.

Or perhaps I am misreading the evidence. The tiny amount I learned about quantum mechanics suggested that underneath the apparently sensible Newtonian universe lies a region of indeterminacy and chaos, where nothing works the way we think it should. So, far from being scientifically ignorant, our leaders may be on the cutting edge of new knowledge. They have decided that not only does the universe not make any sense, but that it *shouldn't* make any sense The uncertainty principle, quite literally, rules.

First broadcast: October 23, 2017

Magical Thinking

The golden age of stage magic coincided more or less with my childhood, which was lucky for me. Not only could we see real magicians performing at the local music hall theater, we could even become magicians ourselves.

There was a magic shop in a nearby town, a dark, atmospheric place full of mysteries. I started out from there with a junior magician's kit and a book of instructions. This was pretty simple stuff like the self-tying handkerchief and the coin through the elbow, and I soon escalated to mind reading and card tricks. My ambition was to master big stage effects like sawing a lady in half. But my only female cousin was unwilling to help me practice, so I never got beyond the small stuff.

All kids love magic. We didn't call it conjuring, we called it magic, and we didn't like the word "tricks" either. "Illusions" was more dignified. But, as a kid, my audience was limited and unsophisticated. "Show us some of your tricks," my aunts would demand at family gatherings, and I would bring out my wand and confound them (and myself) with the linked steel rings, or by making an egg disappear. This last one could be messy. I wasn't destined to become a great magician: I was too clumsy, and too transparent, and I failed to practice enough. In my own defense I must point out that eggs were rationed back then, and my father refused to let me put his valuable rabbits into my trick hat.

Stage magic is in decline these days, killed by computer-generated special effects. Nobody performing live in front of an audience can beat Harry Potter, or even that transparent faker The Great Wizard of Oz. There's David Copperfield, of course, who can make whole jet planes disappear, and Houdini imitators like David Blaine. But movies about magic, like "The Illusionist," tend to place their stage sorcerers a century or more back in time when audiences were less skeptical and the performer's legerdemain was more astonishing.

We do still pretend to believe in magic at least once a year. Primitive superstitions are on the loose in the last dark days of October. Consider how your ordinary supermarket pumpkin, just by being carved into the shape of a face with a candle inside, is transformed into will o' the wisp—the ghost of a long-dead wicked blacksmith called Will Smith, who made a pact with the devil: that's magic. On Halloween, demanding chocolate with menaces becomes a sweet childish game: that's magic. Costumes that disrespect dwarves, witches, werewolves, and people of any and all colors, are accepted as innocent expressions of youthful creativity: that's magic too.

Halloween is an explosion of wishful thinking and political incorrectness. If only magic really worked, how delightful it would be. In a world where science and logic seem to explain everything, I suspect that magic lurks in our minds as a kind of primitive, hopeful faith. Plenty of tricksters take advantage of our nostalgic longing for it. Purveyors of astrology, fortune telling, and miraculous cures are almost as common now as they were in the Dark Ages. Magical thinking has virtually replaced rational thought in Washington DC, and has proven to be enormously popular. It promises a short cut through all the complexities and disappointments of life, straight to our heart's desire. It's hard to resist believing in magic just a little, even though it invariably proves to be a trick rather than a treat.

First broadcast: October 30, 2017

Martin Luther Drains the Swamp

I like to imagine that I am in touch with history, not as a professional historian but simply as someone who has noticed the basic fact that the past shapes the present, just as the present shapes the future. We are the products and playthings of history, whether we like it or not. But the five-hundredth anniversary of Martin Luther's dramatic gesture in Wittenberg in 1517 might have passed me by, if it hadn't been for a flurry of book reviews and an excellent documentary on public television.

This is not the kind of thing we ought to forget. Religious wars over small details of doctrine are still very much with us, but Martin Luther's campaign was more specific. He was protesting corruption which, then as now, was one of the most popular human vices. Human nature doesn't change much, and nobody ever wants to be punished for bad behavior. Most would prefer to be rewarded for it. But in the sixteenth century the prescribed penalty for breaking the rules of the church was very severe indeed—eternal damnation in fact—which is the kind of thing that anyone would prefer to avoid if possible.

This anxiety was an irresistible business opportunity. Agents of the church sold what were called indulgences. An indulgence was a kind of get-out-of-hell-free card that cancelled the buyer's sins. The bigger the sin the higher the price. The practice was abolished in 1567, but still the process sounds strangely familiar: break a law, pay some money, and avoid the consequences.

The desire for forgiveness has never gone out of fashion, although the things we need to be forgiven *for* have changed. Our mortal sins are now mostly about money, and defined by more or less arbitrary human laws. So those who have the power to forgive economic wickedness are our-all-too-human lawmakers. In 1517, as now, if you couldn't afford an indulgence you didn't get one, and presumably paid the penalty in the next world. Now you may pay the penalty in this world, or you may not. Robbing a convenience store of fifty dollars can get you a minimum of five years in jail. Robbing consumers or investors of tens of millions or even billions of dollars may get you some negative press coverage, or a fine, or at worst a well-paid retirement.

You can still buy your way out of trouble, if the trouble is big enough and profitable enough. Indulgences are obtainable from the armies of lawyers and lobbyists who intervene—on behalf of those who can afford it—with the Olympian lawgivers in Washington DC, who alone can forgive out our legal and economic sins, or cancel them out with a convenient piece of legislation. It's not what you do, it's who you know, who you can pay, and how much.

This may be unfair to our political system which, after all, is less corrupt than most in the world. Yet there are so many sinners out there who want to be forgiven, and so many political operators willing to arrange forgiveness for a price, that it may be time for a new Martin Luther, and a new Reformation.

First broadcast: November 13, 1917

Family Secrets

Thanksgiving is quintessentially a family festival. Never mind that improbable story about Indians and turkeys, this celebration is all about families getting together.

Everyone agrees that the family is a good thing, and that "family values" are good values. But families and their values vary enormously around the world. In some cultures a family may include multiple wives and hundreds or even thousands of remote relatives. In others, like ours, it may be just two or three people living in isolation together. Yet every nation and culture has a family system of some sort. We need it as a refuge from the six billion other people in the world who don't know or care anything about us. If our family is small, or nonexistent, or unsatisfactory we can expand it by adding dogs, cats or other creatures. Some of the most valued members of our family are covered in fur. Other people adopt celebrities as imaginary members of their family, some have a quasi-familial relationship with sports teams, or work colleagues, friends or congregations, lodges or drinking buddies. Only the familiar faces, voices and opinions of the family, whoever they are, can give real comfort and security.

Our own family is always the hardest to understand because it is so close that it blurs, and is blurred quite deliberately. When I was young I was intensely curious about our family, but I was always told: "Ask no questions and you'll hear no lies." So I kept on asking questions, and heard plenty of lies, which were always interesting and informative in their own way. In later years I sometimes taught workshops on memoir writing and everyone wanted to write about their family, either to memorialize it as an ideal, or to get their revenge. I encouraged them to dig deep for the truth, but not many were willing to dig at all. Instead they tended to write from their emotional memories, producing either family horror stories of unbelievable nastiness, or Norman Rockwell portraits of perfection. The first type was by far the most interesting, and the somewhat more believable.

Happy families are rather dull. Tolstoy said most famously in *Anna Karenina*: "Happy families are all alike; every unhappy family is unhappy in its own way." A happy family may be a great gift to those who are lucky enough to have one, but it makes poor material for a novel or a memoir. Nobody would want to have Thanksgiving dinner with the awful Lamberts in Jonathan Franzen's *The Connections*, for example, or Mary Karr's ghastly family in her memoir *The Liar's Club*. But we like to read about them. They make our own families seem just about perfect.

If they do seem just about perfect it almost certainly means that we are missing something. Every family has its secrets, and how intriguing they are. When we read the work of a fearless memoirist like David Sedaris, or the English playwright Alan Bennett, we are reminded how much is hidden behind every family's public face. But Thanksgiving is no time to indulge our curiosity. It is the one day in the year when we should listen to our family stories, and believe everything we hear.

First broadcast: November 20, 2017

The Creative Hut

Halfway up a hill behind our local art center there is a small building, a hut or a shed, just big enough to give comfortable working space to one person. It has plenty of windows, and I would be willing to bet that it was built as an artist's studio.

If so it is a perfect example of what I call the Creative Hut, a very ancient device to promote serious thinking. Diogenes, an eccentric Greek philosopher of the fourth century BC, spent much of his time living in a large jar in the marketplace because it helped him to concentrate. Concentration is the operative word A small space blocks out many distractions, and most importantly the distraction of other people. Leonardo da Vinci said, "An artist's studio should be a small space because small rooms discipline the mind." You can't really argue with Leonardo, especially when one of his paintings recently sold for $450 million,

A small space promotes a feeling of comfort and security. You can bet that people who live in those vast houses, like Downton Abbey, Buckingham Palace or in the better parts of the Hamptons, live mainly in a few tiny rooms, and not in their vast echoing halls where nobody could possibly feel at home. Even ordinary domestic houses have a den, a study, or a man cave, some corner where we can retreat for quiet contemplation.

It is almost a romantic tradition for writers and artists to retreat to a shed at the bottom of the garden, or some equivalent, so that they can work in peace. T. E. Lawrence (Lawrence of Arabia) wrote his masterwork work *The Seven Pillars of Wisdom* in a tiny hut that is now a National Trust monument. In 1845 Henry David Thoreau built a hut in the woods near Concord, as a place for solitary reflection. When I wanted some peace and quiet as a child I would retire to the garden shed. I had to squeeze in with the chickens, but they were peaceful companions.

The tradition continues. There is a flourishing business in ready-made Creative Huts. Companies will sell you the entire package, complete with furniture, heating, carpets and electrical wiring, so that your hut is more like a tiny home. But it can't be too much like home, because that is exactly what you are trying to escape. Painful as it may, be the electronic umbilical cord, wired and wireless, should be cut. E-mails, tweets, and idiotic commercial phone calls are all death to creativity, or even to rational thought.

You don't need a literal hut, of course. Our present backyard shed is too full of gardening implements and busy insects for my taste. A cozy room with a "Do not disturb" sign works well, and I have always preferred to work in a small space A car is a good place for thinking, if you are alone, although not so good for painting or sculpture. So is the bathroom, if you can lay claim to it for a while. But any room with a firmly closed door can be a Creative Hut, if you are determined about it. The author Nancy Mitford was famous for keeping the world out when she was working. Anyone making a demand on her would receive a printed postcard with the message: "Nancy Mitford is unable to do what you ask."

There have been creative geniuses, like Johann Sebastian Bach, who could apparently work in the midst of chaos. Most people are utterly distracted by one child, but Bach had twenty children, and managed to compose over a thousand pieces of immortal music. It sounds impossible, and I suspect that, for much of his life, Bach was hiding in his own Creative Hut down at the bottom of his garden in Leipzig, concentrating on his glorious work.

First broadcast: November 27, 2017

Taking the Long View

Nobody can say that things have been dull lately and, as each New Year comes around, we are more or less forced to make a choice between optimism and pessimism about the year ahead. The daily news urges us towards pessimism, which is all the more reason why we should push back as hard as we can.

When this essay was first broadcast in January of 2018 I wrote:

> "Let's admit that, no matter how much we worry and complain, we are lucky to live here and now. If we consider the history of the human race as one big party we arrived at just the right moment. The party is in full swing, all inhibitions have been cast aside, and the drinks have not yet run out. We older folks may even miss the worst of the hangover."

Three years later that paragraph looks positively Pollyannaish. The future always catches us by surprise, and in 2020 the gods who amuse themselves with our fate excelled themselves. No wonder we don't like to think too hard about the future. The word "posterity" has practically vanished from the language. There's no profit to be made out of posterity, and no votes there either. The future is wide open. We can believe what we like about it.

Of course if you are a glass half empty sort of person you will always assume the worst: that it will rain, that the cat will sleep on your clean shirt, that your New Year's resolutions will be an utter failure, and that there will *never ever* be term limits on Congress.

But, with a little creative thinking, we can discover reasons for optimism about practically everything. Our philosophical guide is the character Pangloss in Voltaire's 1759 novel called *Candide or Optimism*. Pangloss held to the theory that "Everything is for the best in the best of all possible worlds." No matter how many dreadful things happened to him—and many did—Pangloss always found an optimistic way to explain them. Even when he was hanged he looked on the bright side.

The secret of optimism is to look beyond petty personal things like death and taxes and take the long view—the longer the better. Consider some of the big things you might be worrying about: global warming, economic collapse, political dictatorship, and computers taking over the world from human beings.

Global warming will resolve one of the great cultural and geographical conflicts of our time. The good people of the American heartland have always suspected that the east and west coasts are little better than Sodom and Gomorrah, infested with atheists and liberals. Global warming will fix this. As the waters rise we coastal people will have to leave the cities, move inland, stop believing in evolution and public broadcasting, and become proper Americans We will all share one culture at last, and only one political party will be necessary, so dictatorship will be the natural system of government. As an added bonus we won't have to move to Florida for retirement. Florida will be under water.

The collapse of the economy under the burden of deficits will allow us to rediscover the virtues of poverty. There will be no more wild credit-driven excesses of consumerism, or outbursts of irrational exuberance on the stock exchange. We will learn to live simple, almost monastic lives out there in the heartland, with fewer possessions, and we will all lose weight.

So don't worry, be happy. Everything will be fine, if we just wait a while. The only cloud on the horizon is the fear that computers will take over the world from human beings before perfect happiness is achieved. I'm afraid it's already too late to worry about that.

First broadcast: January 1, 2018 (revised in retrospect)

You Can Bet On It

My father never gambled, except for a few penny bets on card games with friends. My mother and grandmother allowed themselves what they called "a flutter" on the big annual horse race called the Grand National. But that was only because the queen had a horse in the race, and the bet was never more than their habitual half-crown (two shillings and sixpence). So our family was never in any danger of gambling addiction. I am risk-averse myself, although I will occasionally buy a lottery ticket, as a gesture towards financial planning.

The news that a huge new Casino was planned in the Catskills, and others in Connecticut and Massachusetts, therefore left me cold, although it must have gladdened the hearts of dedicated gamblers in the region. Everything I know about casino gambling comes from old James Bond movies. I have admired the magnificent casino buildings at Monte Carlo and Baden-Baden from a safe distance but was never tempted to enter. A casino, for me, is no more than a trap for upper-class playboys with unlimited amounts of money to throw away, and beautiful blonde young women who are anxious to help them.

Money is hard to earn for most of us, and it seems strange to dispose of it so carelessly without much chance of getting anything in return. But the fantasy of winning is stronger than the dread of losing. Everybody wants to be a winner, although casino profits suggest that the flow of money is almost entirely the other way. It seems that groundless optimism is in our DNA. It must be what encouraged the early immigrants from Europe to cross the Atlantic in the hope of finding an earthly paradise.

Gambling never goes out of style. It was popular in China two thousand years ago, and the ancient Romans were obsessed with it, betting with a throw of the dice on everything from chariot races to gladiators. The mighty Roman Emperor Augustus was an enthusiastic gambler, although he was not himself a casino operator. He lost a lot of money and finally decided that gambling was poisoning the Roman Empire because it drove so many people into poverty. When he tried to ban it he failed completely. Even emperors can't change human nature.

This is an old story. Gambling was illegal and even condemned as sinful in much of the United States until the 1970s. Las Vegas, sin city, was about the only place you could waste so much money so quickly without literally burning it. Then the laws changed and the floodgates opened. Now gambling is not sin, it's fun, it's everywhere, and it's a $250 billion industry. You can't argue with that kind of success.

Gambling has spread through the culture until it virtually *is* the culture, as it was in ancient Rome. Wall Street is nothing but a gigantic gaming house, and most economic policy and personal planning seems to be based on the hope that our winning number is bound to come up sometime so that the debts can be paid off. The business of government, always a gamble at the best of times, seems more and more to be conducted on the lines of a casino. The advertising is shameless, the entertainment is loud and tacky, the odds are stacked against us, and the casino operators are the only ones with luck on their side.

First broadcast: January 15, 2018

A New Royal Family

I sense a growing nostalgia for the idea of monarchy. It is everywhere on our television screens with popular series like "The Crown," "Victoria," "The Coronation," and something called "Game of Thrones" which I haven't seen but which I presume to be a documentary about monarchical politics. Journalists can't get enough of Harry and Meghan, Kate and William. The British royals are fully-fledged celebrities, at least as popular as Justin Bieber or Britney Spears, whoever they are, and with the added advantage of longevity. The average mega-celebrity is forgotten after a few years or a few months, while the royals hang on to the spotlight for hundreds of years. They represent stability, tradition, and a kind of stubborn pride that some people find appealing.

The Presidential system, by contrast, is not looking too healthy on television (consider the series "House of Cards," for example) or in real life. Every year it becomes less admirable, less stable, and less civilized. There must be a better way. If democracy is yesterday's news, there are only two other alternatives: authoritarian dictatorship, or monarchy.

There are forty-four monarchies still functioning in the world Most of them are constitutional—that is the king or queen rules with the more or less willing cooperation of an elected congress or parliament. In fact most modern monarchs have far less power than our President has accumulated in the past few decades, so we're already halfway back to the politics of the Middle Ages.

The main advantages of a real monarchy would not be its efficiency, which would probably no better or worse than the system we have now, but its stability, and relative simplicity. The ludicrous and expensive charade of elections every four years would be unnecessary, and we the people would no longer suffer from the illusion that we can choose between two potential leaders we know nothing at all about. In a single stroke, we could get rid of the political party machines, the primaries, the party conferences, the debates, the ghastly advertising campaigns, the tedious and tendentious speeches, the election itself, and the legal battles afterwards. Instead, we could have a proper royal family, with all the tabloid entertainment that that implies.

But how do we choose them? A simple newspaper advertisement would inevitably produce too many applications from unqualified chancers, narcissists, and psychopaths. We wouldn't want accidentally to appoint another George III or Caligula. On the other hand King Zog of Albania, who reigned from 1928 to 1939, chose himself, and crowned himself, and was a great success. But this is a risky game. Just imagine which of our great leaders might crown himself king in 2020 if he had the chance. No, that won't do.

The younger British royals, as well as Prince Charles, are all unemployed at the moment. They speak English rather well, and might be persuaded to consider a transatlantic career. This plan may already be in progress. Harry and Meghan moved to a luxurious palace-like home California in 2020, in an obvious first step towards the transfer of power. There are several claimants to the throne of France, including Prince Louis Alphonse, the Duke of Anjou, and Prince Henri d'Orleans, the Count of Paris, who might jump at the chance of reclaiming *their* lost colony, and improving our cuisine at the same time.

But that's all in the realm of fantasy. Real life happens only in Hollywood, and that's where we should look for our new royal family. Hollywood alone can manufacture the illusion of style and dignity that we need, with the right background music, and a script that makes at least a tiny amount of sense.

First broadcast: January 22, 2018

Right on Schedule

Some people are incapable of being on time. They start by being born late, then go on to being late for school, late for work, late for dinner dates, late for their own wedding and are only, at the very last, obliged to be on time for their final rendezvous.

This is infuriating for those of us who take pride in being punctual. It is the civilized thing to do, and indeed civilization itself seems to have begun with the careful measurement of time. The Mayans had an elaborate system for keeping track of hours, days, and years, and the five-thousand year old monolith called Stonehenge in southern England is believed to have been a calendar, although not the kind you could hang on the wall. From the earliest days, human beings wanted to measure time perhaps because, like us, they had the uneasy feeling that there was never quite enough of it.

My own schedule is moderately full. Even in retirement the time fills up, and there are things to be remembered every day. So there's a paper calendar hanging on the wall, and I have a little appointment book—a kind of diary of the future—in which I write down the trivial events of my life before they happen: dental appointments, concerts, deadlines, and so on. There's a clock on the wall, and another in the car, and that's about all the scheduling equipment I need.

However, as usual, I am decades out of date. When I have to make future arrangements with more sophisticated people, they bring out their smart phones and we all have to wait through a long period of swiping and tapping and grumbling and showing pictures of grandchildren before we can fix a date or time. Meanwhile I have taken out my notebook and achieved the same result in thirty seconds, thus saving a great deal of—well—time.

The mania for using expensive electronic devices to do what could be done much faster and at a fraction of the cost on paper is, I suppose, a sign of progress, as well as being a miracle of marketing. Now I read about "Apps" for your smart phone (which I don't have) or your smart watch (which I also don't have) that will allow you to program your life down to the last second like a rat under observation in a test laboratory. This neurosis is called "time budgeting" but it might as well be called "life budgeting," and perhaps what these devices offer is an illusion of control over that slippery stuff called time. One such app boasts that (I quote) it will "Show you how busy you are on any given day." But I *know* how busy I am on any given day, it's written on the calendar, and the battery never runs out.

Another way of organizing your life to death is to get one of those fitness trackers, like a Fitbit, that follows every step you take and measures every calorie you use, so that each day becomes a competition with yourself. Nothing is supposed to be done just for pleasure. Everything must be a test. But when I take a walk I want to enjoy the scenery and fresh air, if any, not to worry about meeting some arbitrary exercise standard.

Punctuality and fitness can both be achieved without a microchip anywhere in sight. My age group—the pre-baby-boomers—may be the last generation to understand this, so we should make the most of it. Our time, after all, is running out.

First broadcast: February 5, 2018

Here Goes Nothing

I have been waiting to write about the Bitcoin phenomenon until the whole fantastical pyramid collapsed, revealing the conjurer behind the curtain. But, although the illusion has been wavering and fading recently, I suspect that it may be days or weeks before the final dénouement. So I'll just throw in my electronic two cents' worth anyway, and claim credit for being a true prophet when the inevitable happens.

Money in general is a strange, abstract thing. Most of what we imagine we have is nothing more than a few kilobytes in the memory of a computer somewhere—and we don't even know where. Tangible money comes in the form of little scraps of paper that declare themselves to be "Legal tender for all debts public and private." None of this has any real substance or value, although we behave as if it does. So I suppose it was inevitable that, sooner or later, somebody would dream up a form of money that is invisible, intangible, and more or less indescribable.

We live in an age of illusions. In his eye-opening book *Fantasyland*, Kurt Andersen argues that our economic system is now one hundred per-cent unreality based, as is our politics. Congress juggles with trillions of dollars that simply don't exist, and never will.

There is story, probably apocryphal but often repeated in anthropology classes, about a remote tribe who decided that leaves on trees were money. Those who could climb high enough to collect leaves quickly became immensely rich. But, in the autumn, all the leaves in their forest fell on their heads, and inflation wiped them out. It sounds familiar. There is actually a tribe in the Trobriand Islands that uses yams for money, but at least you can eat yams. Try eating a Bitcoin.

There have been many articles that try to explain how these new cryptocurrencies are created. Their supporters use the word "mining" to describe the process, to reinforce the illusion that buyers are getting something valuable. I would prefer the word "imagining."

Imagining bitcoins into existence takes a lot of electrical power—one single Bitcoin takes enough energy to power the average American home for two years. The only parallel I can think of is Frankenstein's monster, who was also brought to life by a great jolt of electricity. It also reminds me of the paper Monopoly money we played with when we were kids, taking the profits and losses very seriously, and not always playing with complete honesty.

Like our Monopoly money these fragile electronic currencies, are highly vulnerable to theft by cheats and swindlers, and are stolen in the millions, although in a sense nothing is being stolen, because there's nothing there. Only a tiny number of computer obsessives know how this conjuring trick works, but for everyone else it looks very much like a high-tech fraud.

The IRS worries that cryptocurrencies will allow people to avoid paying taxes. But the money the IRS gets now is all imaginary, as is the federal budget. Less imaginary money will make no difference; they can always imagine some more. Cryptocurrencies have been described as a bubble, but a bubble has to have at least some soap around it. They have been described as volatile, but there's nothing to evaporate. Their main purpose seems to be to fuel a secret economy of crime, drugs, and money laundering, which just goes to prove that there *is* no secret economy of crime, drugs, and money laundering. It's all imaginary. That, I suppose, is the good news.

First broadcast: February 26, 2018

Lost in Space

Once upon a distant time I was a great fan of science fiction. If you promise not to tell anybody I will confess that I even wrote a few short stories in that *genre*. But science fiction has gone downhill since its early days, when many writers were intoxicated by the infinite potential of science and technology. There's not much science in science fiction now, not even imaginary science, and precious little about the future either. Fantasy has taken over. A typical story pits brave but puny human beings against mighty forces of evil. I know life sometimes feels like that on a Monday morning, but it is a thin literary diet. The slide from scientific optimism to magical fantasy in a mere half a century is quite disturbing. Let's hope it's not a metaphor of our collective mental state.

Classic science fiction was exactly what the name implies, fiction about science and its possibilities. The central themes were optimistic: the triumph of knowledge, human progress, the conquest of space, and even the end of mortality. Writers predicted many discoveries that actually happened: television, space travel, computers, and radio, predicted in the 1880s by Jules Verne.

Authors like Arthur C. Clarke and Isaac Asimov spun their plots around the question "What if…?" One of my own short stories, for example, featured an invention called the Panacticon, a sort of universal remote control that could command not only the TV, but the weather, the traffic, the growth of lawn grass, the children, the rate of rise of a soufflé, and just about everything except the behavior of cats. This device gave its owner god-like powers, but only so long as she remembered to change the batteries which of course, in my story, she did not.

Science fiction always had a dark side, from H.G.Wells to J.G.Ballard. There were plenty of apocalyptic prophecies, and dystopias featuring the triumph of the machine. These are still very popular, especially in movies. Many young people obviously look forward to the apocalyptic end of the world, and enjoy the ultra-violent previews provided by the film industry.

A big theme in classic science fiction was the intergalactic adventure or space opera. But the real universe has been a bit of a disappointment so far. In the age of Captain Kirk and Luke Skywalker it was positively crowded, although the Hollywood version of outer space suggested that nobody out there, human or alien, had an ounce of common sense. Now we have had a chance to take a closer look at our universe, and it seems empty. But the hope is still there. Even finding a solitary paper clip on Mars would transform our vision of the universe.

The infinity of empty space must surely be populated. One day, I'm certain, we will be contacted by super-intelligent, super-civilized aliens who would like to welcome us into the galactic community of advanced species. They will naturally choose to land in the American capital, which will immediately make them illegal aliens. If and when they can post bail and find a parking space, they will utter the traditional phrase that they learned by studying our old TV shows: "Take us to your leader."

Only a very talented science fiction writer could imagine what might happen next.

First broadcast: March 12, 2018

No Complaints

Nobody loves a complainer. Complaining is a whiny, weak, ineffective habit, not likely to produce any response except irritation. The modern world demands something more. A grievance must be inflated until it reaches the level of outrage, at which point it becomes worthy of media attention. Residents' complaints over (say) broken elevators in a public housing project are not worth a moment's consideration. Anger, outrage, and perhaps violence over discrimination that leaves poor people to struggle up many flights of stairs in summer heat quickly attracts the cameras and the commentators, already pumped up with fury on their behalf—an emotion that is about as real as the passion of an actor playing King Lear.

The news media seem far more emotional and less rational than they were even twenty years ago. Television commentators rage against some injustice or other every day on the evening news. In normal life they are probably perfectly reasonable people, but on TV they are the very incarnation of public indignation about problems that they, and you, and I, cannot possibly do anything about. Like Howard Beale in the movie *Network* they cry: "We're mad as hell, and we're not going to take it anymore." But they do take "it," whatever it is, and do nothing, because outrage is a fire that must never be allowed to go out.

This public catharsis makes readers and viewers feel good. Not only does it tell us what we should be angry about today, but gives us the reassuring feeling that something has been accomplished. How could so much public anger *not* accomplish something? We feel morally improved and self-righteous just because we heard about it, and shared the indignation.

Preachers and politicians use the same device. Synthetic indignation gets people on their side. If some red-faced blowhard is almost apoplectic with righteous anger onscreen there must be a good reason for it. There isn't. The man—usually a man—is out of control, or putting on an act that is all too-well calculated. The trouble with outrage is that it is blind, like loyalty or faith. People performing outrage don't want to conciliate or negotiate, they want to fight. In the end, they often do.

This habit of putting anger center stage leaves the more reasonable part of the population—the vast majority of us—at a psychological disadvantage. We can't very well be outraged about not being outraged. We can't build a winning argument on the basis that things aren't as bad as they seem, or that some modest improvements might be made. Any such thoughtful suggestions will be drowned out by the growls and shrieks of the professionally outraged.

High emotion is exciting, and always bad for us. So let's end with a gem of wisdom on this subject from the eighteenth century conservative writer Edmund Burke, who knew a thing or two about extreme politics, and who lived in a century in which rational thought was greatly valued. He wrote: "Rage and frenzy will pull down more in half an hour than prudence, deliberation and foresight can build in a hundred years." Burke was wrong about a lot of things but, for more than two turbulent centuries, he has been absolutely right about that.

First broadcast: March 26, 2018

The World Really Is a Stage

Italy is a theatrical nation, the home of grand opera and operatic politics, as well as a population who perform life as if every night is opening night. It was therefore not surprising to read about a village near Sienna called Monticchiello in which the inhabitants, every year, stage a theatrical performance in which they act out the dramas and anxieties of their own lives. The script is put together by the community during the winter and then staged in summer with villagers playing themselves.

What a wonderful tradition! Every community has its problems. Big cities have issues that are too vast to put on any stage, but a village could do it, or even a street. Here in the suburbs we have many villages left over from earlier times and still hanging on to part of their old identities. We are lucky enough to live in one, but we don't come together as a community around our shared stories. An office or a school has its own everyday dramas, but out in the disconnected subdivisions people are isolated, without a stage or an audience to appreciate the theater of their daily lives.

In the world of therapy it's called psychodrama—the dramatic public presentation of our own experiences as a kind of catharsis, to make us feel better about them. But we don't need a therapist, we can do it all ourselves like the people of Monticchiello. Even in our one short street we have enough material for a whole season of theatrical events. All we need is a stage and some volunteer local actors and script writers. Citizens could step up to describe or celebrate or lament over the events of the past year so they would by the very fact of being staged take on dramatic significance. It would be the ultimate real reality show, everything local, and everything true.

The weather on Long Island alone in one recent March would provide plenty of material. We had multiple nor'easters, chaos on the roads, railroads and at the airports, the winds, the crashing trees and power cuts, freezing inside our powerless houses, the states of emergency, traffic accidents, the irregular garbage collections, and the disquieting rumble of snow plows in the night. Everyone had suffered, everyone had something to weep and wail about. On the community stage we could let it all out, perhaps with a musical accompaniment from one of the icy northern composers like Grieg or Sibelius, and a few sad songs.

As the winter lament fades away, new scenes unfold. The highways are free of snow at last, but full of potholes big enough to swallow a UPS truck. The skin irritations of winter give way to the allergies of spring, the deer ticks and mosquitoes wake up, and the grass starts growing.

And so it goes and will go throughout the year: the first yard sales, which are a form of theater in themselves, stray dogs, lost cats, deer invasions, traffic accidents, fires. It's all happening here in the suburbs if only we choose to put it on stage: pantomime, melodrama, farce, tragedy, grand opera, soap opera, kitchen-sink drama, and above all the theater of the absurd. One production a year might not be enough.

First broadcast: April 2, 2018

Slow News

When I was a very junior journalist the news cycle was literally a cycle—my form of transportation from one local story to another. The news was delivered as fast as it took me to finish my reporting rounds, pedal back to the office, and type it up. This took some time, but we had plenty of time, and there never was much news anyway.

These days the news cycle is more like a spinning tornado. Everyone seems overwhelmed and exhausted by the quantity and velocity of breaking news, most of it bad and too much of it fake. Stories which, not long ago, would have filled the headlines for a week come and go in a day, before being overwhelmed by half a dozen more. Nobody can keep up with it all. My daily paper has twenty large pages, and yet more information pours out from the television, the radio, and the whole hysterical world of social media. It's too much, far too much.

One response to news overload has been to make reports much shorter—tweets, instant messages, abbreviated web page summaries, thirty-second television reports, and so on. Public Radio news is an honorable exception. In the bird-brained world of tweets and twitters even political announcements with global consequences are reduced to 280 characters, less than the length of a rude joke. Mobile devices, it seems, must never switched off, so this torrent of trivial and not-so-trivial news hammers at our attention all day and all night. It is impossible to actually think about any of it, any more than we can think about the individual raindrops in a thunderstorm.

How much better it would be to make the delivery of news not shorter and faster but slower and more thoughtful. It can happen. I recently learned about a new magazine called "Delayed Gratification," which is dedicated to the idea of slow journalism. Their motto is: "Always the last with the news." I'm glad someone thought of it. Important news needs time—time for journalists to think about it and for readers to absorb it.

In a more leisurely age the news always came late, especially for travelers. Ships on long voyages might find newspapers from home at foreign ports, but the newspapers, along with any personal letters, would be months out of date. Whatever had happened had happened, so there was no point in getting excited about it. This philosophical attitude was destroyed by the invention of the electric telegraph in the 1840s. Patience vanished. Once people *could* know right now they *had to* know right now. Now we *can* know everything from everywhere right now, and it hasn't done us a bit of good. With most news, apart from things like hurricane warnings, time doesn't matter much, or at all. I love getting the news, but I'm never in any hurry for it. I read the morning papers in the evening, or sometimes next day.

News is always new if you haven't read or heard it before, no matter how long after the event. I have taught college students who were quite amazed to learn about the American Revolution. It was as good as breaking news to them.

So I applaud the appearance of this slow news magazine. *Delayed Gratification*, and I wish the publishers well. I haven't actually seen it yet because my first copy hasn't arrived yet. But I suppose that is only to be expected.

First broadcast: April 9, 2018

Little Brother

The Chinese leaders have been reading George Orwell again. They have devised a new plan for what they call "social credit," which will be a ranking of citizens by good or bad behavior. Those with good social credit will receive privileges like better jobs, access to travel visas, and cheaper insurance. Those with bad social credit will have a much less agreeable experience. How will the Chinese government know who's been naughty or nice? By monitoring their internet use. If you interact with the wrong people online, watch the wrong videos, send the wrong messages, or play the wrong videogames, your social credit will go down, and you with it.

This is a tyrant's dream. In his iconic book *Nineteen Eighty-Four* George Orwell imagined a state called Oceana in which citizens were surveyed and controlled by Big Brother, through hidden microphones and cameras everywhere, and video screens on every street corner. China, in one breathtaking step, plans to accomplish the same result without any such vast investment in surveillance equipment. Everyone will carry their own spying device in their pocket or purse in the form of a smart phone, and what's more they will pay for it themselves.

Orwell, writing in 1948, guessed that complete totalitarian surveillance would by possible by 1984, which coincidentally was just about when the first personal computers came on the market. Orwell was a little ahead of his time, but not much. The Chinese government plans to have the universal spying system in place by 2020. Already most of us carry our own self-spying devices which connect to gigantic databases that sweep up all our personal details. Some people have even chosen to install spooky listening gadgets like Alexa and Google Home in their living rooms. If these things don't already work both ways—collecting information as well as giving it—they soon will. Cameras will be next, just in case we are doing bad things quietly. It seems that we are willing to give up almost any amount of privacy for a tiny increase in convenience.

I assume that our leaders in Washington are watching these developments closely. This is clearly the new frontier of political power, the ultimate answer to the vexing question: how can we control all of the people all of the time?

So sometimes I worry that Orwell's dark fantasy has acted not so much as a warning as an instruction book for authoritarian regimes. Stalin's Russia and Mao's China made great use of hidden microphones, as well as armies of secret police and citizen spies everywhere. But the electronic Little Brother in your purse or pocket can do the same job much more efficiently at a fraction of the cost. You could perhaps switch it off, but this is a kind of sacrilege, and the 'off' switch will probably be removed from future models. You could throw it away, but Big Brother will find out and charge you for a new one. The only answer is to do what Winston Smith did in George Orwell's fable: learn to love your Little Brother, and tell him all your secrets.

First broadcast: April 23, 2018

Complicated

Our old television set faded and died. Its replacement was lighter, sleeker, and even cheaper than the old one. But that was the end of the good news. The back panel presented us with a baffling array of about ten different connections with incomprehensible labels. The so-called instruction book consisted of half a dozen pages of flimsy paper, almost entirely safety warnings, with a couple of Zen-like mystical diagrams that could have been anything. The sketchy web site instructions were obviously composed by a man of few words, very few of them English.

None of this was surprising. We have come to expect that any equipment purchase more sophisticated than a paper clip will involve a steep learning curve and a lot of wasted time. After twenty-four hours of struggle and some inappropriate language the TV was working, and the picture was admittedly sharper and brighter than on the old one. But the programs were just as bad as before. Technical improvement and quality entertainment do not go hand in hand. Sometimes they seem to move in opposite directions.

The complexification of ordinary life makes everything more aggravating, more expensive, and slower. Whenever a product or service is advertised as "New and Improved," the truth is the exact opposite. There's even a name for this in England: Hutber's Law, which states succinctly that improvement equals deterioration. Even the geekiest geek quails at the prospect of a new and improved computer operating system. He knows it will take months to get back to where he was before with the old, unimproved system, by which time another improvement will already be in the pipeline.

This process of perpetual reverse improvement has been going on for a long time. When my family first had a telephone at home we simply picked up the receiver and asked for the number. If we didn't know it the operator would find it for us. Now a simple call involves a so-called smart phone, an expensive and fragile gadget the size of a matchbox with about a hundred tiny buttons and no instruction book, no reliable wired connection, no phone book, and no helpful operator. So unless you already know the number, and happen to be standing next to a cell phone tower, you are out of luck. Half the time it doesn't work at all, or sounds like somebody calling from a deep cave on Mars. This annoying gadget has also unleashed a hurricane of semi-literate Tweets on the world, with what may turn out to be catastrophic consequences for the English language, democracy, and common sense.

Our cars, like our phones, have become utterly mysterious, and we can't fix them ourselves any more. On the economic front we must deal with an explosion of criminal activities created by the fashion for using credit cards instead of money: security issues, identity theft, simple theft, firewalls, virus protection, and ever-changing passwords. None of these even existed for the first half of my life, and we managed to live quite well without any of them. If anybody benefits from this it is certainly not the ordinary citizen, whose financial life would infinitely easier if credit cards had never been invented.

There may be a deep biological reason for all this. Complexity is one of the main mechanisms of evolution. We began as single celled organisms that divided and divided until they became a highly evolved and sophisticated creatures impossible to understand, like the Tweeter in Chief. The urge to make simple things more complicated, may be, literally, in our genes.

First broadcast: May 21, 2018

Worth a Thousand Words?

A distant relative sent me a package of old family photographs in the hope that I could identify some of them. It was a vain hope. A few of the images sparked a personal memory: my parents and grandparents, aunts and uncles, and some embarrassing pictures of myself. One of the nice things about human memory is that it is self-editing, and allows us to forget so much. But old photographs can destroy a lifetime of benign amnesia in a single instant. These ancient images brought back so many memories, including our rain-drenched family vacations by the sea, and long-dead aunts outside their long-demolished cottages, a *memento mori* I could have done without.

The oldest prints were unidentifiable. They were faded in more ways than one, thin sepia images with no identification other than frustrating pencil notes on the back like "Jane" or "Grandmother with motor cycle." Judging by the clothes and the cars, these were from the period just before the First World War. If we had a comprehensive family tree it might be easier to identify them, but no genealogist has ever been able to make sense of my ancestors.

If the people in these photographs really were part of my family, they were full of surprises. They showed an unexpected hint of affluence in their elegant clothes and cars. There were some formal studio portraits, including a handsome man dressed and posed like a matinée idol, and one of a beautiful young couple in an ultra-romantic pre-Raphaelite style, as well as less formal family groups. One showed a great crowd of children and adults crammed into a car of 1915 vintage like a bunch of circus clowns. Curiously, some pictures have English backgrounds, and others seem to have been taken in North America. One portrait bears the imprint of a photographer in Canada. I believe the family had a Canadian connection, but what was it? The mysteries multiply.

It is always slightly disturbing to contemplate people from long ago, especially if they have a personal connection. I've never understood why families in past centuries hung large pictures of their ancestors all over the house, watching their every move. It may have been family pride, I suppose, or the need to remind themselves and others of their station in life. But photographs are a private indulgence, not a public statement.

What am I to make of these anonymous pictures? How wrong it is to claim that a picture is worth a thousand words! We *need* the words, just as we do on a painting. What would we make of the famous shot of a sailor kissing a girl in Times Square without the label "VJ Day 1945"? How would we guess that Jackson Pollock's painting "Reflection of the Big Dipper" was about a big dipper, without the title? Obviously we would not.

Without labels this collection of ancient photographs, possibly depicting my ancestors, will remain perpetually anonymous to me. Perhaps they would prefer it that way, and perhaps I do too. Respectable, dignified and mysterious, they represent exactly I kind of ancestors I would like to have had, if I had had any. Sometimes, truth can be death to romance.

First broadcast: June 4, 2018

Polyglot

I have always admired and envied the ability to learn foreign languages easily, or at all. The English language is hard enough, with its half million words, weird grammar, and odd pronunciations. All other languages are worse. When we try to master a new language we are thrust helplessly back to our inarticulate early childhood. I have been to many places where I couldn't understand a word that anybody said: Russia, Hungary, Greece, Mississippi. It's humiliating.

Every summer we see ads for yet another new language learning system, promising fluency within days or weeks just by gazing at your smartphone. These are, to put it mildly, not telling the exact truth. There is no magic bullet. Some people simply have the gift of tongues, just as some have the gift of music or mathematics. We call these natural linguists polyglots. The great critic Edmund Wilson was admired, if not liked, for his ability to read and write fluently in seven languages. But most of us don't have that gift. One language is enough. Judging by some cell phone conversations I overhear, one language can be too much. We are, for the most part, a nation of monoglots and demiglots.

I've been learning French for fifty years with no very impressive result. French is one of the six thousand or so languages now spoken around the world. There's not enough time for me to start on German or Spanish, let alone the other five thousand nine hundred and ninety seven. So when we travel we get by with a few essential phrases learned from a book: please, thank you, how much, where's the bathroom, sorry officer we don't have speed limits where I come from, and so on.

Just to complete this linguistic humiliation, a little phrase book is scarcely necessary. We can simply speak in English, and usually be understood because, in most of the countries of the world, multiple languages are taken for granted and English is the *lingua franca*.

How do they do it? Those wretched foreigners cheat of course. The trick is called education. They sneakily introduce languages into the school curriculum at an early age, and keep teaching them all the way up through college. Very few children escape this regime without a working knowledge of at least one foreign language, and most graduates have two. English is always taught, and this is the downfall of the English speaking nations. We can stumble around the world in a cloud of ignorance, unable to read menus or the local newspaper, but without suffering any real inconvenience because English-speaking locals are always there to help. Why should we bother?

Some people believe that learning languages is the best antidote to intolerance, and idealists still pursue the dream of universal peace through a universal language. Unfortunately some of the most murderous wars in history have been fought between peoples who shared the same language, so this may not be the answer to anything. But if there is ever a universal language I hope it will be English, as nature and Hollywood intended, although it is just as likely to be Chinese, or Spanish, or Arabic. It will depend on who wins the wars of numbers—economic numbers and population numbers—and it would be a shame to waste years studying the wrong language. I'll just wait and see.

First broadcast: June 18, 2018

The Makeover

A steady stream of advertising material clutters up our mailbox. We are told that the average American, whoever *s/he* is, sees five thousand advertisements every day, so it must be hard for advertisers to break through the clutter. One sneaky trick they use is to include your own name in a prominent position. Nobody can resist their own name. An example came the other day, a card with the bold headline: "Time for new makeup, David?" Well, I thought contemplating my face in the mirror, it probably *is* time. Perhaps some of these chemicals in the pretty jars and pots, illustrated on the card, would improve my appearance and make me look younger, or at least different.

Our favorite French village is quite small but has two beauty parlors, which may be just what I need. But my wife won't let me go near them. "Not for you," she says, which seems unfair in this age of sexual equality and gender fluidity. I wouldn't mind giving it a try.

It seems that nothing defines us so much as our desire to be something else, which may explain the impulse to dress up at Halloween, and weddings, and other occasions when anonymity may be useful. We love the idea of the makeover, the dramatic transformation, the sudden effortless leap from one state of being to another. There's nothing new about this. The Greek myths are full of transformations although, because the ancient Greeks had a pessimistic view of life and fate, the transformations were often of a negative kind. The gods could change themselves into animals, birds, or humans, and sometimes got stuck in that inferior state. Often the gods and goddesses transformed other gods or mortals to punish them. Daphne, the beautiful daughter of a river god, for example, was demoted into a laurel tree, Narcissus and Hyacinthus became flowers. It wasn't much better in Biblical times. Lot's wife was turned into a pillar of salt for some minor infraction of the rules. Shakespeare loved to play with transformations, as when the weaver Nick Bottom was turned into a donkey in *A Midsummer Night's Dream*.

Our more optimistic culture gives a positive spin to the fable of the instant makeover. Some of our most popular legends and fairy tales are about an ordinary person who, through luck or magic, turns into an extraordinary person. Men become gods or heroes, women become (astonishingly often) princesses, like Cinderella, Prince Harry's wife, or pop stars. In the Wizard of Oz the Tin Man, the Scarecrow and the Cowardly Lion all dreamed of getting a makeover, although they didn't need one. Batman, Superman, and all the other super-heroes and super-heroines dreamed up by Hollywood are appealing precisely because of their chameleon quality.

But now the dream of instant self-transformation seems to have escaped from the fantasy world, and is propagating like a malicious virus in real life. It has morphed into TV shows like American Idol that promise instant celebrity, and endless makeover shows that offer advice on fashions, plastic surgery, fitness, fatness, and even good manners. Now the shows have expanded their realm even farther, instructing us how to makeover our homes, our gardens, our children and even our pets. Nothing is immune from this rage for sudden and dramatic improvement except perhaps the mind. I haven't heard of any TV shows that claim to improve the *mind*, although a brain makeover is what many of us most urgently need. I myself would like to be smarter, younger, taller, and thinner, in that order, but nobody is offering that particular package deal.

The myth of the instant effortless makeover is enormously seductive. But if magic fails there is always the slow road. It's called re-invention. Unfortunately this is hard work, and it takes time, but a lot of people do manage it. Scott Fitzgerald wrote that there are no second acts in American lives, but how wrong he was! Think of Ronald Reagan. American lives are all about second, and third, and fourth acts. *The Wall Street Journal* even has a regular column called "Second Acts" that has featured a Bay Area defense attorney who became a college track coach, a Telecom executive who started a fashion handbag business, and a banker who became a chef. One of the champion self reinventors is Rosey Grier whose odyssey took him from pro football with the LA Rams to being a TV personality and singer, a Christian Minister, and an expert on needlepoint.

The end result of self-reinvention is every bit as dramatic as a makeover, and it last longer, and you learn something in the process, and you can still recognize yourself in the mirror afterwards.

First broadcast: June 25, 2018

The Pleasure of Rituals

Everybody knows what to expect on The Fourth of July. There will be flags, barbecues, picnics, concerts, parades, fireworks, political speeches, and the Post Office will be closed. In a world so full of uncertainties it is good to be sure of something. Every nation has some such annual festival. Polish National Day May 3 is marked with folk dances, traditional costumes and lots of food, on Saint Patrick's Day the Irish like to wear green, go to church, and watch rugby matches, and the National Day of England, April 23, is treated with complete indifference, which is a kind of national ritual in itself.

We humans are a ritualistic species. We love grand national events like the Fourth of July, and even international ones like the Olympics or the G20 summits. The distinguishing feature of these events is that they are soothing because they are always the same, like a religious service. If you look at photographs of world leaders at the G20 over the past few years you will see that, although the leaders have changed, the pictures are always identical, as are the results of the meeting. These are symbolic moments: they are not events designed to achieve anything, they are rituals designed to make us feel better.

We never quite escape the gentle embrace of ritual. Except for a brief period when anarchy reigns, between the onset of adolescence and the arrival of common sense, most people's lives, including mine, are repetitive to a degree we don't even care to think about. The repetitive routines of work and suburban life, from commuting to lawn care to cat feeding, get us through the day, the week and the year without the need to make complicated choices. They symbolize normality. This what everybody expects, so this is what we do Sports and games are entirely ritualistic, as are graduations, weddings, elections, pop concerts, riots, wars, and medical checkups. If everyone plays their part there are rarely any surprises. Rituals keep us on the rails, and the training starts early. I remember being sent off to school as a five year old, every day at what seemed to me like crack of dawn, and complaining loudly that I would much prefer to go at a time more agreeable to myself, or not be sent at all. But this was the ritual called "education" and my protests were ignored. So I slept through every morning at school, which is another ritual.

The popular philosopher Alain de Botton has written a lot about the importance of rituals in our lives. In a book, provocatively titled *Religion for Atheists*, he argues that, in some important sense, what religions believe is less important than what they do, and what they do is to bring people together through shared rituals. I say that he "rediscovered" this idea because, almost exactly one hundred years ago, the French sociologist Emile Durkheim proposed it in a book called *The Elementary Forms of Religious Life*. It was true then, and it is just as true now. Why do we keep doing the same things in the same way over and over again? Because it feels good. Why does it feel good? Because it connects us to other people who are also doing the same things. For once, if only for a day or a moment, we are all in harmony.

First broadcast: July 2, 2018

There's a Hole in My Bucket List

Many famous travelers of the past like Lord Byron, Robert Louis Stevenson, and Gertrude Bell were essentially solitary. That was how I started out in my teens, puttering around Europe on a motor cycle. I was alone not because of my noble independent spirit but because nobody was brave enough to ride on the back. Now we travel in crowds, sometimes crowds of two or three thousand when a big cruise ships comes in. There's no "escape," whatever the Sunday Supplements tell you, and precious little wonder or magic in that kind of travel.

Tourism, almost everyone agrees, has become a kind of plague. It's not that there's anything wrong with the desire to explore new worlds and new civilizations. It's just that everybody wants to go to the same places at the same time. These approved "sights" may not be the most interesting places to see, but they are always the most crowded. We are all travelers now, but only in the sense that UPS truck drivers are travelers: we cover a lot of miles and make a lot of stops. But the miles become increasingly repetitive and the stops increasingly predictable until the awful realization dawns that we are in danger of getting bored. The tour companies invent more extreme and exotic destinations and activities every season, but it's a small planet. We may be running out of things to add to the bucket list.

My own bucket list is almost empty. It seems to shrink naturally as one grows older, and perhaps an empty bucket list is one of the gifts that comes with age. No more nightmarish airports, no more excruciating guided tours in the blazing sun, no more penitential hotel beds, no more picturesque ethnic restaurants that send you straight to the hospital. Now I'm inclined to let young people do it. That's what young people are for: to go to war, or to go to Florence—experiences that are not totally dissimilar.

I am no longer intimidated by popular guide books with titles like *A Thousand Places to See Before You Die*. At the most generous estimate, I have seen no more than two hundred and eight of the essential thousand, and I have been to dozens of places *not* on the "must see" list and have therefore wasted my limited time. If I were to take these guides seriously I would have seven hundred and ninety-two indispensable places still to visit. The Great Colonnade at Palmyra in Syria was conveniently destroyed by ISIS, but that still leaves the Borobudur monument in Java, and the Tsukiji Fish Market in Tokyo, and seven hundred and eighty-nine more. This would mean, by my calculation, about eighty trips a year, or almost two a week, and I'm just not going to do it.

I am confirmed in this resolution by a dream I once had in which the world supply of oil ran out suddenly without warning. The planes stopped, the big cruise ships stopped, the cars and coaches stopped, and everybody was forced to stop wherever they happened to be at the time, like a global game of musical chairs. Astonishingly, the dream came true in 2020 with the coronavirus pandemic. If you were lucky, you were marooned on Paradise Island. I was marooned comfortably at home. But an unfortunate cousin of mine was marooned for three months in a hot hotel room in Amritsar, India. I can no longer face that kind of existential uncertainty. My bucket list is closed.

First broadcast: July 9, 2018 (updated February 2020)

Ancestor Worship

Genealogy, the study of family history, has been around forever. Royal and aristocratic families existed only because they had, or pretended to have, a line of distinguished ancestors stretching back into the distant past. Just knowing who your mother was, which is all most of us think we know, wasn't enough to claim a place at the high table. The right ancestors were essential, and the role of the genealogist, in every age, was to find the right ancestors, whether they existed or not.

Ancestor worship was and is common in many cultures, and we still have traces of it in our own. When we are young the ancestors hang over us like a dark, disapproving cloud. Curiosity about them stirs only when we are older, and can imagine becoming an ancestor ourselves.

There was a time when family was destiny and ancestors meant everything. They still do if you happen to belong to one of the royal families of celebrity, politics, or money. But, for the rest of us, what we hope from our ancestors is that they may shine the oblique light of their distinction on us, if they had any distinction. In this sense genealogical research is a kind of self-esteem therapy. If I can find someone illustrious in my family line they would reflect glory, however dimly, on me. No such ancestor has yet come to light, but you never know. Consider how many people claim ancestors who came over on the Mayflower. That boat must have been the size of several modern cruise ships.

This particular kind of personal history never appealed to me, even as a child. Occasionally I think about my honorable ancestors, but not for long. I suspected that my family was a bit peculiar, and that the less I knew about them the better. Genealogy is like archaeology—most of the really interesting stuff is buried deep beneath the surface. The portions of my family visible above ground, so to speak, didn't offer very great hopes that digging down into the past would produce anything impressive, or even respectable. The only person with my family name who ever made it into the history books, Sir John Bouchier, signed his name on the warrant for the execution of King Charles I in 1649, which may be seen as a good or bad thing, depending on your opinion of monarchy. Years ago, some incautious research into my father's side of the family came up not with French aristocrats as we had hoped but with a family of unsuccessful French circus performers—probably clowns.

Yet there seems to be a national craze to find our roots, driven by web sites like Ancestry.com and TV programs like the "Generations Project;" " Who Do You Think You Are?" And the "Genealogy Roadshow." Fortunately the discoveries made by genealogical research are usually so vague and uncertain that they can safely be ignored. If you like the conclusions you can embrace them as true, especially if something heroic or romantic comes up. If the search reveals nothing but peasants and petty criminals you can safely ignore it.

This is all good, innocent fun. What surprises me a little is the popularity of DNA testing, a kind of biological selfie, which seems to offer a scientific shortcut to the past.

The problem with science is that it might give you the right answer, instead of the answer you want. DNA only reveals traces of ethnicity, as far as I understand it, but even that can come as an unwelcome shock to some people. The companies that provide this service claim that it can point you in the right direction for further genealogical research, discovering your tribe as it were. But if you turn out, like most of us, to have mixed origins, a lot of expensive ancestry tourism may be involved in the follow-up A friend of mine describes himself proudly as "Half Chinese, half African, half Scottish, half South American Indian, half Welsh, part Barbadian, Trinidadian, and born and bred Guyanese." He travels a lot.

Nobody wants to discover ordinariness in their past, although the vast majority of people always had ordinary lives. The chance of hitting the ancestor jackpot is small. Your Great Great Great Great Grandfather may have crossed the Delaware with George Washington in 1776, but it's much more likely that he was chopping wood in some Appalachian backwater at the time.

But if the ancestors are disappointing there are always the descendants. In fact I suspect that we are seeing a cultural shift from ancestor worship to descendant worship. The extraordinarily intense focus on children is surely something new. Back in the days when people revered their ancestors, children were of little account and were largely ignored. Instead of ancestral portraits hung on the walls, now it is children who are photographed and videoed every minute, their images displayed in the house, e-mailed to relatives, posted on FaceBook, and applied to greeting cards. It's clear that they, not the ancestors, are at the center of the family universe. These soon-to-be-exceptional children shine the light of distinction as it were backwards, from their future success. Anything can happen in the future, so pride doesn't have to wait. And, after all, children *are* the future, and ancestors are the dead past. But the ancestors had one advantage: they offered a reality check. If they had no distinction we could forget about them and focus our attention on the present. As Voltaire said, "Do well in this life, and you will have no need of ancestors."

First broadcast: August 18, 2018

Eyes Down

I admit to having a mild phobia about new shoes. It dates back to childhood, when every school year began with a new pair of regulation lace-up leather shoes, with a choice of black or black. After a summer of bare feet and sandals our feet had to be broken in to these new shoes, and we hobbled about in agony for the first two weeks of school, taking small, careful steps like elderly invalids and sliding like ice skaters on the smooth leather soles. Two years in army boots did nothing to improve my attitude towards footwear and, since those days, I have bought shoes very rarely, choosing the most comfortable ones I can find, and wear them for a long time.

Yet a lot of people of both sexes are passionate about shoes. Long Island has shoe stores the way Saudi Arabia has sand. There are a dozen outlets in the local mall, all overflowing with shoes and boots in a vertiginous selection of styles and colors and sizes and widths, more than the whole population of Long Island could wear out in a dozen lifetimes.

Even more mysterious, at least to me, is the popular love affair with sneakers. I have always thought of these as footwear for those too young to wear proper shoes, although of course adults these days are much younger than they used to be. Sneakers are virtually a cult. There are books about them, collectors spend serious money on them, and there is even a sneaker a museum in Boston. Murders have been committed in pursuit of especially desirable sneakers. They are, it seems, a kinds of fetish in the anthropological sense. A fetish is an object that is believed to contain mysterious power. In ancient times all kinds of objects were believed to contain this power—statues, amulets, carvings, bones, and so on. The Egyptians worshipped cats, the only part of their strange religion that made any sense.

One of the most astonishing pictures to come out of the Coronavirus epidemic was published in *The New York Times* in June 2020, the day after a few stores in the city had been allowed to reopen. It showed a (very) long line of potential customers waiting to get into an establishment called the Foot Locker. All were young males, all were wearing sneakers, some were poking their feet through the barricade to show off their sneakers, and all were taking a significant risk of infection and death in order to buy—or at least to gaze at—more sneakers. If that's not religion I don't know what is.

There's nothing sinister about this. Freedom of religion is the bedrock of this nation's Constitution, and fashion is just one religion among many. But why shoes? I don't go around staring at people's feet. Do you? It could be dangerous, you could walk into things. And feet are the least noticeable part of a person, being right down there on the ground, below display level, as it were.

But something has changed. Shoes have become more visible. So many people walk around with their eyes focused down on their smart phones that they must be seeing more of their own feet than they did before, and other people's feet too. The Chinese have dubbed them the "heads down tribe," and have even created special walking lanes in some cities to avoid accidents. The heads down tribe can hardly avoid glimpsing shoes and sneakers down there on the sidewalk all day long. So one addiction can feed the other.

I am fortunate not to own a smartphone, but I tested this theory with a borrowed one. It's true, you can look at your phone and watch your feet at the same time. What I also learned from this exercise was that I was wearing a very disreputable pair of casual shoes that I had bought in Portugal in 2005, and that had not improved with time. Perhaps I might need a new pair?

If the smartphone addiction is all a commercial plot to sell shoes, it is a diabolically clever one. Fortunately, as soon as I had returned the borrowed smart phone to its owner, I forgot all about shoes and carried on with my pedestrian life as if nothing had happened.

First broadcast: September 10, 2018

Intelligence Test

It has been reported, but not much discussed, that Norwegian researchers have discovered that intelligence, as measured by standard IQ tests, has been declining since 1975. I had been wondering about this myself, especially for the past couple of years. In the national league table of IQ tests, America comes in ninth, slightly behind Norway. In case you hadn't guessed, Hong Kong and Singapore come in first. America's average IQ score has gone down at about the same rate as in many European countries, which seems to suggest that intelligence is on the decline across the western world. Thinking is out, feelings and emotions are in. What's going on?

I'm not smart enough to figure out the reasons myself, but experts have speculated that the apparent decline of intelligence may be due to less rigorous teaching methods in schools, and to the rejection of reading in favor of semi-literate video entertainments. There's no simple answer, and nobody can even agree what exactly intelligence tests are supposed to measure. There are many kinds of intelligence, including emotional intelligence that may be more valuable in real life than the kind that solves academic puzzles.

By the time you get to my age you should have come to terms with your intelligence, or lack of it. We have not been tested for a long time, we have probably forgotten or repressed the result, and we don't expect ever to be tested again. So it is tempting to feel a bit smug about this apparent decline of brain power in the younger generations. It just confirms what every senior citizen believes. Sex, drugs, rock and roll, and the internet have fried their brains.

But I had a chastening experience this summer in France. It's true that France is a more intellectual nation, where even the bookstores can give you a headache. But normally the casual visitor doesn't have to think about this and, of course, *not* thinking is what most of us do best.

I didn't escape quite so easily. My French teacher—I am sure with the best of intentions—gave me as an exercise the task of answering a list of question from the philosophy section of the *Baccalauréat* or "bac," an examination that French students take at the end of high school. Now I'm no intellectual but I do claim to know a little about philosophy, and I wasn't afraid of a few questions designed to be answered by eighteen-year olds. Not until I looked at them. Try these.

Question 1: "Does culture make us more human?"

Question 2: "Is desire a mark of our human imperfection?"

Question 3: "Can one be indifferent to art?"

And ten more questions like that, along with this *coup de grace*: "Is truth final?" All these had be answered in four hours, in essay form. There are no giveaway multiple choices.

To be sure, these were questions posed to students who had been taught and prepared at school to expect them—but still, teenagers. I was tempted to dodge the test by pretending a sudden illness or a mental breakdown. But in the end I went ahead and answered the questions as well as I could, and in French of course just to make it harder. My answers made the teacher laugh, but only with amazement. She confirmed that I would certainly have failed the exam, as she expected and as I expected. But 88% of teenage students passed this same examination this year, which makes me wonder: whose IQ is really in decline—theirs or mine? The correct answer is not one I want to hear, in French or any other language.

First broadcast: July 17, 1918

The Annual New Start

New Year is a strange liminal date, full of anxiety and hope and empty resolutions. The inescapable change of the calendar makes us feel that something important should happen, but what? Where do we go from here? Are we looking forwards with hope, or backwards with nostalgia? In 1825 John Quincey Adams admonished the nation to "Think of your forefathers! Think of your posterity!" That's not the kind of message we want to hear nowadays.

The past was a time of dreadful technological backwardness. Our wretched forefathers didn't even have cell phones, and we wouldn't want to be like them. As for posterity, the people who will come after us, nobody worries about them anymore. Posterity is history. The economy is a Ponzi scheme, already $20 trillion in debt, our perpetual wars are not going well, nature seems poised to deliver some painful lessons, and politics has taken a great leap backwards into the rude and ruthless 1850s. It's not surprising that we prefer to turn our backs on all that and focus on ourselves. That's where New Year's Resolutions come in. We may not be able to control the great tides of politics and economics, any more than we can control the rising tides of the ocean, but we can at least take charge of our own personal lives.

This is a notion that can apparently survive any amount of disproof. We all know people who have been making the same resolutions about diet and exercise and smoking and drinking for decades. Their resolutions are always consigned to oblivion by Easter, and often as early as Valentine's Day.

This is because we make the wrong resolutions. They tend to be punitive and puritanical, rather than prescriptions for pleasure. Diet and health resolutions are doomed before they start. In fact, polls show that fewer and fewer people *are* making New Year's resolutions these days. It may be that, after long experience, we have lost faith in our power to change or that, quite sensibly, we are less inclined to inflict pain on ourselves. To that extent, we've become more realistic, or cynical if you prefer.

A resolution is a way of pressing the personal reset button. It doesn't have to be a discipline or a strait jacket. In fact, it shouldn't be. The etymology of the word "resolution" stems from the Latin verb *solvere*, meaning to loosen or reveal, or set free.

In that spirit my resolution is to set myself free from negative resolutions, and give myself the gift of a positive one: to take more pleasure in small things, to become more naïve, to indulge a few whims. The older we get, the more we tend to find the world tedious and predictable. I would prefer to move in the opposite direction, so that I find everything interesting, new, and fun.

So I'm not giving up anything next January. Instead I'm adding a few things that I pretend I never had time for: some classic novels that I forgot to read, some very gentle Tai Chi exercises, writing longer and more interesting letters to my friends, and trying to see them more often, keeping the bird feeders filled, and cleaning the car at least twice a year. Wish me luck.

First broadcast: December 31, 2018

Small Worlds

It seems that the algorithms that increasingly rule our lives have decided that I am getting younger as I get older. For years I've been hounded by advertisements for arthritis remedies, hearing aids, lounge chairs, river cruises, health insurance, and other useful products for senior citizens. Now, suddenly, I have crossed another invisible barrier and entered my second childhood. The latest catalog to arrive in the mail with my name on it is for toys.

Admittedly these are rather old-fashioned toys, not suitable for today's children. For example they are non-electronic and do not flash or beep, which means that no modern child would even look at them. But they certainly bring back memories of my own youth, and especially the picture featured on the catalog cover of a miniature steam engine. I had one of those once. It was only about eight inches square but had all the essential working parts: a boiler, a piston, and a flywheel. When the water was heated by a spirit lamp—always a risky procedure—the engine would get up steam and the flywheel would begin to turn slowly, then faster and faster until it ran out of steam and stopped. It didn't do anything else, and the absolute uselessness of my little engine enchanted me. It seemed like a profound metaphor of something, perhaps of life itself, but I was too young to comprehend just how profound it was.

The rest of the catalog was full of models of the kind I always loved: cars and trucks, planes and boats, trains and space ships, and even an exact scale model of a classic Triumph motor cycle that I actually owned, full size, back in 1959. Here, in miniature were all the means of escape and adventure that young boys—and I'm sure young girls too—dream about.

Many hobbyists of all ages create miniaturized worlds that are better-organized and more manageable than the real one. You can buy little houses, like doll's houses, with tiny people and animals to match, and even trees and fences, to construct your own small utopia, a solid three-dimensional world that has more substance than a computer graphic. It is extraordinarily appealing, and I was really tempted by that motor cycle. It may seem silly, but it's hard to believe that such hobbies are nothing but a substitute for life. They are so obviously about the life we really *want*, where everything is exactly right, and where we are completely in charge. The absolute power of the hobbyist over his tiny world can be strangely attractive.

Looking through my catalog of models I was reminded of a classic science fiction story by Eric Frank Russell called "Hobbyist." The haunting premise of the tale is that we ourselves and our planet are nothing more than the miniaturized creations of some unimaginably remote cosmic hobbyist, who makes worlds and sets them in motion purely for the fun of it, just as we might play with a model railroad or a toy village. The story gave me the creeps because I thought: doesn't life feel just like that sometimes, as if we are the playthings of some crazy, inhuman hobbyist, perhaps in a distant galaxy, perhaps much closer? But how would we know? Of course we wouldn't, and we don't.

First broadcast: January 21, 2019

Strange Encounters

Perhaps the most curious phenomenon of tourism is the journey to see an event or situation that no longer exists, and perhaps never existed. This strange behavior is as old as history. Pilgrims have always journeyed to places where religious visions might or might not have appeared, or famous people might or might not have been buried. But the ubiquitous cellphone has given this activity a new dimension of strangeness. The goal is to visit nonexistent sights and to photograph them, preferably with one's own face in the foreground. But more than that it is about participating in the world of movies. Tourists want to visit a place where something was once filmed in order to film it again, minus whatever made it interesting in the original film.

Here's an example. The small village of Porthothnan in Cornwall, England was used as the setting for a popular romantic TV series called "Poldark," based on the ultra-romantic novels of Winston Graham. The stars and camera crews have long since departed, but the village is inundated and almost choked by fans to come to see where the stars *had been*, and take pictures of the empty beach and the empty harbor. Another victim of this strangely vampiric form of tourism is Dubrovnik in Croatia, used as background in Game of Thrones. The small port is absolutely overwhelmed by camera-toting people who perhaps imagine that they are taking a trip back to the Dark Ages and might meet the ghost of Lord Eddard. Millions go to Hollywood to see where old movies were made, and walk the streets where forgotten stars once walked.

On a more humble level a home repair show called Fixer Upper has made the small town of Waco, Texas famous, as if it wasn't famous enough already. Over two million visitors have made the pilgrimage. Everybody who has attempted to do real home improvement knows that it is just about the most tedious and unromantic task in the universe. But on television, apparently, it's magic.

The magic of the screen is powerful. Pilgrims, for that's what we must call them, come from great distances and go to great expense to experience the unreal unreality of what isn't there. Visitors travel all the way from China and Korea to photograph some chalk cliffs in England that were once featured in Harry Potter, although Mr. Potter himself was no more than a clever illusion.

This is all perfectly harmless, of course, unless you fall over an English cliff or drown in Poldark's romantic cove. But it is interesting because it shows how many people believe that movies are somehow really real, and that celebrities really are extraordinary human beings. This is deep, supernatural pagan stuff, but not hard to understand. It is a quest, in the historic sense of the word—like the quest for the Holy Grail. It's a perennial theme from *The Epic of Gilgamesh* and Homer's *Odyssey* all the way to Indiana Jones and *Lord of the Rings*. The child in all of us loves a treasure hunt and, when we grow up and discover that all the real treasure is locked up in other people's foreign bank accounts, we may look for a purpose in the larger-than-life world of movies. These tourists are on a quest for something seen but unseen, real but unreal and, unlike the heroes of ancient times, they usually find what they are looking for: the very place where the illusion was created. Then they can take a selfie, and become part of the illusion themselves.

First broadcast: January 28, 2019

Time after Time

Several years ago I gave up wearing a watch, not because of any metaphysical uncertainty about the nature of time but simply because the band began to irritate my wrist. I tried all kinds of bands—leather, plastic, metal—and eventually took to keeping the watch in my pocket, like a nineteenth century gentleman. But then, I suppose, I had a kind of epiphany. Did I actually care what time it really was, all the time? Some watches are status symbols, but mine wasn't. If I had been accosted by a street mugger he probably would have looked at my Timex with contempt and given me *his* watch. Now, at least, I could avoid that embarrassment. I put my watch away for good, and didn't even buy a smart phone as a substitute because I didn't want to exchange one kind of slavery for another.

But I never got the chance to enjoy my disconnection from the twenty-four hour alarm clock of life, because it never happened. Clocks are everywhere. Looking around the room where I work I find two clocks linked to the atomic clock in Colorado that tell time to a microsecond, one regular old battery-driven clock, one clock on each of the two computers, and I just noticed that there's one on the telephone screen too—a total of six in a room fifteen feet square. A count around the rest of the house revealed nine more, plus one in the car. All of them are ticking down the seconds, minutes and hours to…what? The apocalypse? The 2020 election? Brexit? Lunchtime? Or to something we don't want to think about? We don't know because we can't see the future, no matter how many watches we have or how expensive they are. But at least the ticking bomb of time is not physically strapped to my body.

Time may not be a good joke, but it is certainly a joke of some kind. The general theory of relativity, insofar as I understand it which I don't, suggests that time is cosmic joke played on us by the nature of the universe. The theory suggests that time is not fixed but relative, in which case *nobody* knows what time it really is. This fits with our everyday experience. We all understand at some level that time is relative. A two week vacation goes by in a flash whereas an hour on a hard seat in the Department of Motor Vehicles can stretch out for years. Your clock is a deceiver, like your bathroom scale. Yet the world seems absorbed and obsessed by clock time, and how to defeat it. In the days of sailing ships it took up to six weeks to cross the Atlantic. Now an hour of delay at the airport sends travelers into a frenzy of rage and anxiety.

Putting away my watch has not freed me entirely from the tyranny of time, but it has had a calming influence. Clocks and watches fix our attention always on the future, and what is going to happen next. But we can never get ahead of time, because it always ends right here, right now, and the future is still in the future. It's a moving frontier, or a wall if you prefer. We can never sneak through it or see over it. Once we realize this, we can relax. As for the future, if we accept the wisdom of the highest authority, we'll see what happens.

First broadcast: February 4, 2019

The Valentine Contract

In the final week before February 14 about half the population is worrying about what to do for Valentine's Day, while the other half doesn't understand what all the fuss is about. It's a difficult time, for romantics and cynics alike. The avalanche of red hearts, chocolates, sentimental cards, and expensive flowers that precedes Valentine's Day can turn your heart to mush, or to stone. Either way the event itself is likely to be a disappointment. Unlike the Super Bowl, Valentine's Day rarely produced a clear winner. It's more like English cricket, which usually ends in a draw.

Valentine's Day began in the 1800s as a special day for lovers, and would-be lovers. Things were very intense back then, between women and men. You only have to read Jane Austen or Charlotte Brontë, or watch any one of a dozen historical romances on TV, to appreciate the enormous importance attached to the intersection of money, love, and marriage a hundred and fifty years ago.

We still attach enormous importance to money, love, and marriage. These themes dominate television soap operas, the pop music scene, and the huge romantic novel market. Never has love been so intensely promoted, and never has it been so difficult to find in real life.

The problem is that romantic love takes time, and nobody has any time. This explains the enormous success of online dating services that cut through the tedious business of finding Mr. or Ms Right and bring two hearts together electronically, with a minimum of time wasted. Even seniors citizens know that they don't have time to find love the old fashioned way. The impatient over sixty-fives unwilling to settle for a book by the fireplace have their own online dating services, with millions of subscribers.

Romantic love depended on suspense, distance and mystery. Long courtships were common, often carried on by letter, and sex was only a remote fantasy. Now there's no suspense, no distance, and no mystery. Once the computer has brought them instantly together, lovers are as closely connected as any married couple.

But we don't have problems with love just because of high-speed technology or our busy lives. We have problems because we don't know what it is any more. Not only do women and men define love in different ways, but *everybody* defines it in different ways. You will love our burgers, says the fast food industry, and we are constantly invited to love cars, pop stars, smart phones, and floor wax, among many other things. The President, during his campaign, liked to open his arms and say "I love you people." Well, yes, I'm sure it's true, but love in the twenty-first century takes some strange forms.

Because nobody understands love, if they ever did, it has been largely replaced by the term "Relationship" (with a capital R). A Relationship can be just about any affair that goes beyond a single night in a ski resort motel. A Relationship is more like a contract, which everybody understands. You can ask: is it is it enforceable, is it fair, do I lose or gain by it? Such questions rarely occur to the heroes and heroines of romantic stories.

The chilly legalistic language of Relationships makes one almost nostalgic for romantic love—the old-fashioned uncontrollable eternal kind that didn't fizz out like a cheap firework on February 15 but lasted, if you were lucky, the entire year.

First broadcast: February 11, 2019

Please Don't Give Me the Facts

In the year 1660 a learned society was founded in London by a small group of men who believed that science and scientific method could reveal all the secrets of the universe. The motto of the society was *Nullius in Verba*, which those of us who failed Latin at school might hesitantly translate as "Take nobody's word for it" or, in the words of Sergeant Joe Friday in the ancient TV series Dragnet, "Just gimme the facts." This motto showed the determination of scientists to resist arbitrary authority, and to verify all statements by facts based on experiment.

It was an auspicious time for a scientific enterprise. The dictatorship of Oliver Cromwell had ended, and a relatively tolerant king, Charles II, was restored to the throne. In 1663 the king gave his patronage to the learned society of scientists which became and has remained The Royal Society. Benjamin Franklin was one of its most distinguished members.

Not everybody loved the new society. There was a great deal of ridicule in the newspapers, and its meetings were sometimes broken up by rowdy mobs of know-nothings. Indeed, some of this early science seemed ridiculous because the scientific method was still in its infancy. Jonathan Swift in *Gulliver's Travels* satirized imaginary experiments like the extraction of sunbeams from cucumbers. But if you don't have any facts, scientifically speaking, any crazy thing is possible, and the only way to find out the facts is by systematic observation and experiment.

The fear and rejection of science has a long and dismal history. Every age and culture has its own ways of explaining the world, and people naturally resist the suggestion that what they think they know is wrong. But that's what science does, relentlessly. Galileo was the most famous example, with his improbable idea that our little planet was riding a kind of carousel around the sun, but there are tens of thousands of other examples of science that provoked angry denials, all the way from Semmelweis's discovery of the causes of infection to Darwin's theory of evolution to present day campaigns against vaccination and climate change theories.

There are always those who would prefer not to know the facts when the facts may cause political problems or reduce profits. Politicians seem more fearful of science than others, perhaps because its method demands definite answers to definite questions, which is the definition of a political nightmare since politics is all about evading questions.

This is an old and indeed an ancient story. Greek mythology offers an image of human nature as divided between the Apollonian and Dionysian. Apollo is the god of rational thinking and order, who appeals to logic, prudence and honesty Dionysus is the god of wine and dance, of irrationality and chaos, who appeals to emotions and instincts. The two natures co-exist in us, and the tension between them is either tragic or creative, according to which philosopher you choose.

We seem to be tilting rather too far in the direction of the Dionysian character that hates and fears the cool hand of science. How refreshing it would be to have a leader, or a whole government of leaders, who took as their motto *Nullius in Verba*, or, as Joe Friday might have translated it, "Just gimme the facts."

First broadcast: February 18, 2019

Lost in Translation

Language is a tricky thing. I started talking when I was about three years old and I'm still talking, usually in what I believe to be English. Other people talk to me in the same language. Yet scarcely a day goes by without some kind of misunderstanding, usually trivial, about what somebody has said, or meant, or implied. Unfortunately I learned an older, more primitive version of our language and, as Oscar Wilde remarked, Britain and America have everything in common except their language, so everything is translation for me. It's not just a matter of different words, like French fries for chips, but of style and emphasis. British English tends to understate some things just a tiny bit, while American English overstates everything to an amazing, incredible, and extraordinary degree.

Everyone knows this, but it gives cause for concern about those big international meetings where important things are decided between people who speak *completely different* languages, and are linked only by an interpreter. Translation, especially simultaneous translation, is a highly skilled art, and far from infallible. Split second decisions about the meaning of words can make a big difference.

Adding to the difficulty, not every negotiator is even good at understanding it or speaking his own language. English is a complicated and subtle tongue, and has a huge vocabulary of words that are frequently ambiguous. How often do we grope for a word, and find exactly the wrong one? Sophisticated language skills are essential in negotiation, which is why a highly disciplined form of diplomatic language arose in the thirteenth century and why, for four hundred years, the language of diplomacy was the same all across Europe. Every educated person spoke French as well as their own language, so no translation was needed.

Diplomatic language, which is a kind of translation it itself, is not only for diplomats. It is essentially the same as polite language, and it oils the wheels of human relationships. How many wars, divorces and, bankruptcies have been precipitated by the wrong word at the wrong time? We need an inner censor, because the uncensored mind is often crude, hasty, and thoughtless. Our whole civilization is based on *not* saying what we think. But it is precisely these evasions and delicate shades of meaning that cause problems in translation.

It is impossible to guess how many funny, silly, and sometimes catastrophic misunderstandings may have happened in international meetings over the years. One famous example was the statement by Russian President Nikita Khrushchev in 1956 that was translated as: "We will bury you." This turned the heat up on the cold war, but what he really said, in Russian, was: "We will outlast you," which sounds far less threatening. The Bible is a translation of a translation of a translation of an oral tradition, and scholars have been disagreeing over what it really says for a thousand years. Men have been burned, beheaded, or have gone to war over one interpretation or another.

We depend on the interpreters, those fragile human links, to get it right, and must hope that that they don't have agendas of their own. The fact is that we don't know, and we can't know. We can only trust that those who negotiate in important international meetings understand the pitfalls of translation and, when it comes to the big decisions, follow the wise advice of Theodore Roosevelt: speak softly, and carry a big dictionary.

First broadcast: March 4, 2019

Please Wait

If your computer is like mine one of the first messages that pops up on the screen when you try to get started, is "Please Wait." This is the mantra of the modern age. My old typewriter never told me to wait. But if we are foolish enough to use the automated checkout at the supermarket we rarely get far with our groceries before being stopped by the message: "Please wait, help is on the way." Oh no it's not. Help is out to lunch. Please wait.

It is a poignant reminder that, while we imagine we are living in the fast-moving world of the twenty-first century, there is nothing fast about it. We have been trained and bullied into waiting for almost everything. If you make the mistake of travelling during the summer you will probably waste most of your vacation time waiting at airports: waiting to check in, waiting for security, waiting for your flight, waiting for your in-flight meal, and, at the other end, waiting to disembark, waiting at passport and customs barriers, and waiting for your bags to arrive on the carousel, if they ever do. Standing with an impatient crowd at JFK recently I calculated that, during my longish lifetime, I have, at minimum, spent the equivalent of five days and nights waiting at baggage carousels

Waiting is one of those universal human afflictions that we rarely think about. Only the very rich never have to wait, while the rest of us spend uncounted hours on checkout lines, in doctors' offices, at the DMV, or on hold for some more-or-less imaginary "customer service representative." We do this passively, with resignation. There's rarely a rebellion, although perhaps there should be. Waiting is time lost forever, and we never get a payback or a refund, or even an insincere apology.

In some ways technology has reduced waiting time. We used to wait for the mail, but now we have instant electronic communication. We used to wait for packages, but now Amazon delivers them, it seems, even before they were ordered. The microwave and fast food industries have reduced the time between the desire to eat and eating virtually to zero. But for most things in life we have to curb our impatience, and please wait.

There are two kinds of waiting: passive and active. The passive kind is forced on us by circumstances and is always for the convenience of other people or machines. Active waiting is something we choose to do. There are those who make a profession out of it: security guards or tree farmers for example, who have nothing to do but wait. Others wait for pleasure, like fishermen who sit on riverbanks for hours at a time in a state of Zen like tranquility.

Some people make an entire lifestyle out of waiting, as if the present moment was a kind of prelude or prequel to some anticipated big moment in the future. Samuel Becket's play "Waiting for Godot" is the classic drama of hopeful waiting. The two tramps on stage are waiting for someone or something that will make everything right for them. They discuss their situation endlessly, and even contemplate hanging themselves, but they can't manage even that. The tramps put a kind of genius into their waiting and it's clear at the end of the play that they can't stop. Waiting is what makes their lives worth living. It gives them something to do when they have nothing to do. They have learned resignation, they have learned patience. We should all be so lucky.

First broadcast: April 24, 2019

The Kindness of Strangers

During some recent travels I was suffering from a bad knee. It was nothing serious, but just one of those things that happens when you keep using your knees for decades without any proper maintenance. But it made me even more unstable on my feet than I normally am, so I plucked a nice solid walking cane out of the umbrella stand by the front door and started using it to help me get around. Problem solved.

The un-anticipated results were astonishing. All my life I've seen people walking with sticks or canes, sometimes with crutches, and always felt a twinge of sympathy for their slowness, their awkwardness, and what I assumed to be their pain. But I never expected to carry a walking cane myself, just as you never expect to get white hair or special offers from the AARP. In the nineteenth century a stick was part of every gentleman's attire, along with a hat. Both were partly protective measures against the blackguards and master criminals who infested the streets in those days, as anyone knows who reads Sherlock Holmes stories. My stick, I told myself, was like this: a fashion statement with defensive possibilities.

But everyone else took it seriously. It got me to the front of every line, including the passport line and the boarding line at the airport. I knew in a general way that airlines had employees whose job it was to help the disabled, passengers who needed wheelchairs, passengers with small children, and so on. But I hadn't expected them to appear out of nowhere and help *me*, which they did, with smiling courtesy.

I felt like a complete fraud. I was by no stretch of the imagination disabled, just a bit unsteady on my feet. But the cane was clearly a signal for the helpers to swing into action, and I was too embarrassed to refuse the small privileges that came my way.

It wasn't only the airport personnel, whose job it is to help. *Everybody* seemed eager to help. I was offered a seat or a steadying hand by kind people more often than I can count. You won't believe this but, as a pedestrian, I was even waved across the road by *French drivers,* and they weren't joking. They actually waited for me to cross.

We all need help from strangers sometimes, often unexpectedly, and they need help from us. It was good and somewhat shameful to be reminded of it. I can remember when boy scouts (I'm not sure about girl scouts) were encouraged to do a good deed every day, like helping old ladies across the road. I was never a boy scout myself, but I didn't want to be outdone by them in the matter of good deeds and often tried to help old ladies across the road, although sometimes they put up a stiff resistance. Now, I suppose, this particular good deed is redundant. All the old ladies are driving huge SUVs, and I need protection from *them*.

In a magazine designed for elderly people I read the claim that a walking cane, with the aid of a technique called "cane fu," can still be way of frightening off robbers and muggers as it was in the nineteenth century. Properly flourished it will cause them to drop their guns and knives and run. I have not yet had the occasion to try this yet, and hope not to.

I still have my cane, but resisted the ignoble temptation to invest in some crutches. Very soon, no doubt, my knee will be healed and I will be restored to my old more-or-less steady self, needing and deserving no help. But being helped was heartwarming, and I will miss it. How do you signal to the good Samaritans of the world that you have a bad back?

First broadcast: August 5, 2019

The Image

I was preparing to take a photograph of an attractive buildings in a French village when a little girl popped out of her doorway and asked: "Why are you doing that?" in excellent French, considering how young she was. I had no ready answer, in that or any other language, but it was an interesting question. Why was I doing that? She may not have understood that I was simply taking a picture. My big, old, black camera looks more like a death ray machine than the colorful toy-like cameras she grew up with. But either way she had, like any child, gone straight to the heart of the matter.

Why *do* we photograph perfectly commonplace places and things? Before photography came along artists would sketch and paint the scenes they saw on their travels to show to people who had never been there. But now everybody *has* been there, and taken their own pictures, and there are billions more pictures in books and on the web, so what's the point?

I could claim, but honesty forbids, that I was photographing this village scene for artistic reasons. That particular building on the corner has an attractive combination of colors, textures, curves and angles that makes it visually appealing. But nobody has ever accused me of having artistic reasons for anything.

So why *was* I doing that? My camera is too heavy to hold at arm's length, so I don't take selfies and in any case I know what I look like. On the other hand I have always regarded a camera as a portable memory. We have the old-fashioned habit of keeping a photograph album, which is now such an archaic object that it has become the subject of one of those nostalgic documentaries on public television. We have a library of albums as big as medieval Bibles, in which our memories are carefully preserved. The pictures have scarcely changed over the years. The main actors get a little older and grayer, but the prints are so small and fuzzy that it scarcely matters. Photograph albums give a reassuring sense of time standing still. Unlike a smart phone they also keep your false memories safe for decades and decades.

In a photograph album the great world is reduced to a manageable size. At 4" x 6", every place looks pretty much like every other. The labels are missing from many of our older pictures. Here are some impressive but unremembered ruins that might be in Greece or Detroit, unsteady portraits of parties and party animals long forgotten, picturesque country scenes that could be anywhere. These mystery pictures have a special charm. They allow the imagination to work.

So was I taking this photograph for the family album? Not really, we have several pictures of the same place already. The girl was waiting for an answer to her question, her little arms folded in the classic pose of exasperated impatience. When we are very young I suppose we do imagine that grownups know what they are doing and why. It's only later that the awful realization dawns on us that grownups have no idea. They are just pretending, improvising from minute to minute.

"I'm not really sure" I said feebly. The little girl stared at me with contempt, and vanished back into her house, confirmed in her opinion that all foreigners are stupid. When I consider her still-unanswered question, I fear she may be right.

First broadcast: August 19, 2019

Real Work

It is a paradox that Labor Day is devoted to fun and idleness because it is the one-day in the year when we are supposed to celebrate *work*. In particular we should be honoring the history of the Trade Union Movement that protected workers and gave them a political voice.

Work is not popular any more, at least not what my father would have called "real work," where you get your hands dirty, use your muscles, and maybe even sweat. Most young people wisely prefer an office job, where the most challenging physical task of the day is switching on the computer. There is plenty of strenuous physical work to be done, but there is almost no connection between the value of that work and the rewards for doing it. We need plumbers much more often and more urgently than we need pop musicians or politicians, but guess who stands higher on the pay scale.

A reminder of this unwelcome fact came in the mail the other day. We get a lot of strange catalogs. I regularly get one for industrial packaging, for example, and another for heavy lifting machinery, although I don't have much use for industrial packaging or heavy lifting machinery. The catalog that came just in time for Labor Day was for tools, so I looked through it. I already have several tools—screwdrivers, hammers and so on—and I could always use more.

But these were professional tools for big jobs: massive

generators, super-sized pressure washers, high-capacity pumps, hydraulic power packs, air compressors, high-powered bench tools and, yes, heavy lifting machinery—four hundred and ninety six pages of equipment designed for serious work. If there's anything calculated to give a sedemtary man a feeling of inferiority it's a catalog like this. I once talked to the owner of a tool rental company who told me that suburban men often like to test their masculinity by renting tools they can't handle, like chain saws or pneumatic drills, and have to be dissuaded for insurance reasons. He dissuaded me from renting a digging machine that I certainly didn't know how to handle.

Under all the semi-mystical claptrap about computers and virtual reality is the fact that we live in a physical world, a *built* world, and somebody had to build it. The most exquisitely sensitive poets needs a solid roof over their heads, but few of them would know how to construct one, any more than I do.

Studs Terkel, in his wonderful book of interviews called *Working,* reported conversations with many real workers. One said, in a proud phrase that stuck in my mind, "We built the pyramids"—meaning that workers just like him built the pyramids, and everything else

We owe a lot to the workers who really work, often with hard-to-learn skills and hard-won experience. Without them we paperwork professionals might have to work ourselves, which scarcely bears thinking about. At the very least we should spare a thought once a year on Labor Day for the men and women who really *did* build the house we're sitting in, the power lines that run our computers, the barbecue grill, the bridges we cross on the way to visit the family, the swimming pool and, yes, everything.

First broadcast: September 2, 2019

Stormy Weather

The unpredictable cruelty of the weather led our ancestors to assume that it was sent by capricious gods to torment us mere mortals, or perhaps just for their own celestial entertainment. This theory has persisted for thousands of years, and it makes perfect sense to me. Weather forecasting, in spite of satellites, super-computers and sophisticated modeling techniques, remains almost as fallible as stock market forecasting. The weather will do what it will do. Spring turns suddenly into high summer, and a delightful autumn snaps brutally into winter. It makes no difference whether it was forecast or not.

Weather is infinitely variable, like life itself. We want to predict it and to understand it, but it always takes us by surprise. Forecasts, at best, are good for only a few hours. On the other hand weather is just about the only thing we think we can predict *at all*. So those fanciful forecasts occupy a disproportionate amount of time on TV and radio news programs, and are often delivered with operatic exaggeration as if they were real news. Then life goes on as before—warm or cold, wet or dry, as the case may be. What have we learned? Nothing.

There are three distinct types of weather. The first is what might be called social weather, the universal topic of conversation. Mark Twain complained that "Everybody talks about the weather, but nobody *does* anything about it." That is precisely why weather is such a reassuring subject, because we *can't* do anything about it. It is fate. Sometimes I call friends in Europe and we invariably talk about the weather there, and the weather here. We enjoy these conversations, and hang up the phone with the feeling that we have exchanged important information. The weather on the south coast of England is wet and cold. The weather on the north shore of Long Island is warm and wet. It's something we can share.

The second type of weather is what I call public relations or fantasy weather. You find it in tourist brochures, glossy magazine articles, and guidebooks. This weather is always splendid, and it's all lies. Every traveler knows this. Promoters of tourist destinations never tell the truth about their weather. When you get to their tropical paradise in the middle of a snowstorm they always claim, without much conviction: "This is very unusual."

Thirdly we have weather as drama and entertainment, which is where the hurricanes and storms come in. For serious weather junkies the Weather Channel offers twenty-four hours a day, three hundred and sixty-five days a year of meterological *schadenfreude*. Eighty five million households subscribe to the Weather Channel, which offers a steady diet of hurricanes, tornadoes, floods, and other extreme weather events, usually affecting unfortunate people who live far away.

But sometimes fate catches up with us and dramatic weather arrives right here where we live, so it's hard to ignore it. Then weather forecasts are no longer boring. The meteorologist becomes our prophet and our lifeline, and we wait anxiously for the true word. Are we all doomed, or just some of us? There's not much we can do about extreme weather except to stock up with cat food, candles, and long Victorian novels. But at least, for years into the future, it will give us something interesting to talk about.

First broadcast: September 9, 2019

Under the Influence

I read a magazine article about young people who make pots of money by becoming "Influencers" on the Internet. The idea of making pots of money without any real work has always appealed to me, although I have never succeeded in actually doing it. The "Influencers" described in the article, though rich, did not seem to be especially talented or intellectually gifted, so I thought there might be a *niche* for me in this new industry.

Those of us who are behind the times and understand nothing important may need a little explanation. An Influencer is (and I quote the Delphic Oracle of our times, Mr. Google) "A person with the ability to influence potential buyers of a product or service by promoting or recommending the items on social media." The majority of Influencers are celebrities, who are no doubt deservedly famous for being famous. But there are many more who, less celebrated, are called Micro Influencers.

I decided that I would fall into the second category, Micro Influencer, because my influence is very small and even cats pay no attention to my suggestions. But the influence required is not of a moral or behavioral kind, such as influencing a cat to get off the couch. It is more of an economic kind, a matter of persuading people to buy products, or "brands" as we cutting-edge Influencers like to call them. So I need to find a brand to promote, something that I buy myself and can recommend. This is not easy, because. I don't buy very much and most of what I buy is rubbish. This past weekend, for example, I purchased four large screws from the hardware store, a forty pound bag of bird seed, and some toothpaste. I fear that my consumption patterns may not be glamorous enough to excite the online crowd.

Also—and this may be a serious obstacle—Influencers apparently lurk only inside smart phones and on what I call the anti-social media, places that I never visit. I suppose I could get one of those smart phones, there is a shop nearby that sells them. But I make very few phone calls, for which I use my phone at home. It has a wire attached and works perfectly, but doesn't seem to have the right features for Influencing.

This electronic illiteracy may be why I have escaped the influence of the Influencers so far, although I am sometimes influenced in other, non-electronic ways, as when I choose a book to read from a review for example, or buy food in the supermarket, where my choices often depend on our domestic Influencer-in-chief, namely my wife.

It may be that, without these new Influencers and all their slippery ancestors in the advertising and PR industries, all the way back to P. T. Barnum, we can never hope to know what to do, what to eat, where to go, or what to wear. The choice, after all, is more or less infinite, and I feel I have been left behind by this exciting new cultural development. Suppose I decide to buy something? How will I know what it should be? I need an Influencer I can trust, a paragon of taste and discretion who understands my preferences, my limitations, and my budget.

This seems to leave only one option. I must abandon the hope of getting rich by influencing others, and find a way to influence myself.

First broadcast: September 16, 2019

The Sounds of Silence

One of the more serious stories to make it into the newspapers last summer was the saga of Maurice the rooster. Vacationers on the island of Oléron in south-western France had complained that Maurice's daily wake-up calls had ruined their sleep. They did more than complain, they sued the rooster's owner in court, claiming the bird was a public nuisance. Thousands of French people signed a petition in defense of Maurice and, after a long legal process and a great deal of lighthearted publicity the judge ruled in his favor. A rooster has the right to crow, said the judge, it is in his nature. Maurice became quite famous, just for doing what nature intended. He even had his picture in *The New York Times*, twice, and quite right too.

Vacationers often make dumb choices. They look for relaxation in some quiet rural place but, once they are there, they miss the sounds of the big city—the roar and screech of traffic, the sirens, the screams and the gunshots that make up the background music of their urban lives. The deep countryside is profoundly quiet at night, to the point of being scary, but you can get used to that. What gets through to even the most insensitive brain is *unexpected* noise in the midst of silence, and that was the crime of Maurice the rooster. In the quiet dawn hour a rooster's wake-up call crashes in like an artillery shell, with shocking effect. "I'm awake, how about you?" he seems to shout. The farmers and the hens sleep through it all, of course. It's just like gunshots or sirens to them.

We *can* sleep through almost any amount of noise, if it is familiar noise. I once lived right next to a main railroad station in London that generated a shattering decibel level, day and night. But I slept there like the proverbial baby. The same was true when we lived in a French village where the church clock, just a few yards away, chimed the hours and quarter hours loudly and relentlessly for twenty-four hours. Once we got used to it, it was as good as a sleeping pill.

The general rule about noise seems to be that animals should be quiet, but humans can make as much as they like. It is part of being Lords of Creation I suppose. But do we need to be such *noisy* lords? Lawn mowers, leaf blowers and all the machinery of what I call 'backhoe gardening' make the quiet suburbs almost intolerable at times. A boom box car drives past our house about midnight every night, shaking the windows. The boy who drives this car must wake hundreds of people every night—I suppose a judge would say it is in his nature—and my only consolation is that he will soon be deaf.

I'm rather sensitive to human noise myself, but try to tolerate natural sounds. A night time cat chorus doesn't trouble me, they need a social life too. But sometimes my tolerance is tested. The other night, after the boom box car had passed, an owl started up right outside our bedroom window. He was a barred owl, an impressive bird with a spooky and penetrating cry. He had lot to say, and he kept on saying it. I told myself that the barred owl is a fine fellow who deserves his moment on the stage. But at that moment, just for a moment, I could sympathize with those sleep-deprived French vacationers who wanted to make a casserole out of Maurice the noble rooster.

First broadcast: September 30, 2019

Good Advice

Nothing is more annoying than good advice. But when it comes from an unreliable source, like one of your relatives, you can dismiss it out of hand. Just to take one example: all through my childhood I was told by my mother and my numerous aunts that, if I got wet, I would catch a cold. Well, I got wet almost every day on my way to school, and I had a cold for years. It seemed like an open and shut case of cause and effect. Decades later I read that research had proved conclusively that nobody can catch a cold just by getting wet. My colds came from school, where we had so many viruses on the loose that it was virtually a biological warfare establishment. My mother refused all her life to believe this, and always tried to prevent me from getting wet.

Everybody likes to give advice but nobody likes to take it, including me. Whenever I am given a piece of good advice I immediately pass it on to somebody else who will benefit from it more, and I suggest that you do the same. Giving advice is satisfying only to the giver, and there have been thousands of advice books published since ancient times. George Washington himself wrote one on etiquette. But we seem to be living in an age when nothing can be done without first seeking advice, and it has gone way beyond books. The internet has made it a thousand times worse. Anyone, with or without qualifications but with a video camera can post their own instructional video on anything from extreme Tai Chi to building a bomb. There may be as many as a million of these sites, nobody knows. The bar of expertise is set so low that I've been tempted to launch my own advice column, or even a video, offering advice that I know for certain to be reliable. For example: how not to get wet when it rains; how to change your typewriter ribbon; how to talk to your friends without using the internet. We're all experts now. My guess is as good as yours.

The impulse to give advice could be a heartwarming example of human generosity and unselfishness, except that the advice often leads, directly or indirectly, to buying some product or embracing some idea. Disinterested advice is hard to find

Much of this information is self-cancelling because every piece of advice generates an equal and opposite piece of advice, and usually they're both wrong. This seems to be as common in science as it is in religion or politics. Fortunately the self-proclaimed experts on any subject usually divide into two camps, rather than ten or fifty. This makes our choice much easier, like chocolate or vanilla. But we still have to choose. Mixed advice is particularly annoying when it concerns health: eggs are good, eggs are bad, sunshine is good, sunshine is bad, and so on. Experts disagree as much in medicine, where supposedly they have some hard facts, as in politics or religion, where facts are nonexistent. Expertise has become a matter of faith rather than knowledge. It's not that the advice givers know better, but they *think* they do and have the self-confidence to say so.

Most of us will choose the advice we like best. This is my own philosophy, and I suspect that of everyone else on the planet shares it. If I am told that spinach is good for me I dismiss the idea out of hand on the grounds that the research is inadequate, and probably funded by the Spinach Growers' Council. If I hear that red wine is good for me, I assume, without further investigation, that the research is one hundred percent reliable.

One of the many things that annoys me about all this is that nobody ever asks me for *my* advice. I have plenty to give, on almost every subject including (and especially) those I know nothing about. But on the rare occasions when I suggest a beneficial lifestyle change to someone I know my proposals are greeted with incredulity, or amusement, or both. It seems that anonymous characters on You Tube are more to be trusted than a real, non-electronic person standing right in front of you. My advice, for what it's worth, is to beware of advice and, if you think you have any advice to give, keep it to yourself.

First broadcast: October 21, 2019

Yesterday's News

We once had the habit of recording good television programs on videotape. This was back in the days when there *were* good programs, and before videotape become obsolete. If you have done this yourself you probably made the same mistake we did, recording programs you didn't want because the timer wasn't set properly, or because you forgot to stop the tape. Unlike DVR recordings, which eventually have to be deleted, videotapes stick around on bookshelves or in boxes for years and decades, becoming an accidental archive of recent history.

In this careless way we have accumulated regular library of programs that we never intended to preserve. Many of them are segments of Public Television news, and it comes almost as a shock to rediscover them. They remind us how many enormously important events we have completely forgotten, almost as if they weren't important at all. How quaint the recent past seems when viewed through the reverse lens of television: Charles and Di on the road to divorce, Bill Clinton on the road to ruin, Newt Gingrich riding high, John Glenn coming down to earth. Then there are the eternal themes that have appeared in every news medium since news was invented: earthquakes, floods, tidal waves, and wars, always with the same pathetic images of the victims.

The news media present every predictable disaster with an air of surprise, as if nothing like it has ever happened before. But it has, and it makes you wonder about what we count as "news," and how much it matters. I admit to being a news addict. But when my wife asks me: "Anything on the news?" I usually have a hard time remembering the main stories of the day. There are always reports of trouble in the Middle East, epidemics in Africa, political corruption at home, bad weather somewhere, nasty crimes, medical horror stories, and celebrity weddings and divorces. But the particular details of today's stories blur in the mind because they were essentially the same yesterday, and the day before. This may be the reason why some elderly people keep heaps of newspapers going back for decades. They are tangible proof that nothing has changed.

In some ways the sameness of the news is reassuring, like an old familiar song. On the rare occasions when real news happens, like 9/11 or the COVID-19 pandemic, the effect is absolutely shocking. Imagine how nerve racking it would be if every day's news was so totally unexpected. Imagine waking up to stories of corporate generosity, government honesty, celebrity modesty, and peace and goodwill among men. We couldn't stand the excitement.

"Yesterday's news" is a synonym for dead, dull, useless information. But yesterday's news was today's news yesterday, and we consumed it as avidly as we always do. It's easy to imagine that, in ten or twenty years' time, we may find an old digital recording full of today's most thrilling news, and look at it with the same bemused curiosity. Why did we think any of that was important? Yet some of it *was* important. In the relentless daily flow of news there are some things we really need to know, stories that have the potential to change our lives. We just don't know which ones, until it's far too late.

First broadcast: November 18, 2019

Hunting and Gathering

I enjoy reading history, and particularly those grand, ambitious books that sweep up the whole human race into a single narrative. It is all very well to learn exactly how many troops assembled in what order at the Battle of Brandywine Creek in 1777, and exactly what weapons they carried, but that is such a tiny part of the human story, a footnote to a footnote. I like to contemplate the whole picture. It puts our present obsessions in perspective.

The first such mega-narrative that came my way was H.G.Wells's *Outline of History*, originally published in 1920, which starts from the origins of the earth and goes on from there. More recently I've read the highly successful book *Sapiens* by Yuval Noah Harari. The title refers to our particular species, labelled by anthropologists as *Homo sapiens*, or intelligent man. This name, though flattering, scarcely seems to describe our chaotic and irrational species in the twenty-first century. We need to find a more honest label for ourselves.

The least intelligent thing we humans ever did was to take up agriculture, and subsequently gardening. We all know in a general way that humans once lived as hunters and gatherers. They moved constantly from pace to place, subsisting on what the land provided.

About ten thousand years ago a great change happened. People began to settle in one place, and to grow crops and raise animals. They became farmers. This agricultural revolution sounds peaceful and bucolic, but in fact it was a change from a free life to a very restricted one. Farmers can't roam, they are tied to their land and the limited diet it can produce, and they are guaranteed a lifetime of back-breaking toil while being highly vulnerable to attack from bandits and stronger tribes. Hunter gatherers can always move on to new territories.

Nevertheless agriculture remained the common way of life for thousands of years, and when we look at the gigantic farming industry we might assume that nothing but the scale has changed. But everything has changed. Only two per-cent of the population now works on the land. Ask yourself why the highways of Long Island and Connecticut are packed with traffic even in the middle of the working day. The drivers are obviously not working. Indeed it sometimes seems that nobody is working at all, and the offices and factories must be standing empty. The fact is that everyone has gone back to hunting and gathering. We call it shopping, and it is our central, absorbing life activity, just as it was for *Homo* more-or-less *Sapiens* ten thousand years ago. Even food is still collected in the old, haphazard way by grazing from one fast food joint to another, reproducing the varied diet of the ancient hunter gatherers: fried chicken one day, tacos the next.

Hunting and gathering may sound like an uncertain way of life, but shopping is even worse. There's so much more stuff to gather—no longer just roots and berries but plastic trees and musical toilet rolls and decorative socks, and a million other made-in-China treasures. It may be that, with our strange human genius for getting things wrong, we have created the worst of both worlds: trapped by our real estate like farmers, but forced to be constantly on the move looking for stuff, like hunter gatherers.

The only consolation is that history moves in circles. When the fuel runs out, and there's nothing left in the shops to hunt or to gather we may find ourselves living the simple life, back on the farm.

First broadcast: December 2, 2019

A Short Walk in the Woods

The view from my window is bleak in winter. The small patch of woodland behind the house has been exposed by the falling leaves as a very small patch indeed, not much more than a hundred feet wide. After November it is nothing but a thin screen of bare branches, and I can see right through to the next undistinguished suburban house on the other side.

Autumn may be a pretty season, but the fall of the leaves reveals landscapes of almost unbelievable dreariness. We need those trees, but we are getting rid of them as fast as we can. It's a rare day when the buzz of chainsaws can't be heard somewhere in the neighborhood. Homeowners worry, with good reason, about falling trees that may demolish their houses or cut their power. Developers are nervous about falling profits as the last scraps of land are used up. Trees are an obstacle to the march of suburban progress.

Woods and forests have been vanishing ever since man discovered fire and invented the barbecue. But in the past few centuries it seems that we have been trying to finish the job and create a desert. Long Island was once ninety per-cent forest. Most of that forest has been turned into suburban homes like ours with pine kitchen cabinets, and polished wood floors. There are still big oak trees a few feet from my window. But a hundred years ago there was probably one growing exactly where I am sitting now, which is an uncomfortable thought.

It is more than just a matter of preserving pretty landscapes. Research in the last few decades has revealed more about the qualities of trees as living things that help to clean our air, and perhaps can even communicate between themselves in vast, mysterious underground networks. Woods are part of our culture, magical places outside of civilization. Hansel and Gretel are forever lost in the forest. Shakespeare's fairies and spirits inhabit them as their own. Robin Hood rode out from the green woods to crusade against income inequality. Every other television mystery you ever saw features characters being pursued through the woods, lost in the woods, burying bodies in the woods. Without the woods there would *be* no mysteries.

We are lucky to have our state parks. But we should also treasure the remaining scraps of woodland that make our suburbs look a little less like those in Arizona. Even these small clusters of trees are full of life. There's a whole wild menagerie in the quarter acre patch behind our house: birds and squirrels, bats and mice and rats, voles, moles, rabbits, and an occasional deer passing elegantly through—it's their natural habitat, their last remaining space in the ever-expanding subdivisions. That's why a wood, especially at night, can seem so otherworldly and strange. It is haunted by the dark, whispering trees, the busy nocturnal lives of the animals, and all the witches and elfin spirits who have lived there throughout history. Lawns, highways and strip malls are *our* natural habitat. Woods belong to another dimension.

The shriek of the chainsaw is more than just noise pollution, it is a kind of assassination. Sometimes, reluctantly, we may have to take down a dangerous tree, but it always involves a moral struggle and it's all our own fault. The trees, were here first.

First broadcast: December 16, 2019

Everybody on Stage

Acting was once a marginal occupation. In Shakespeare's time actors were considered not much better than vagabonds, and even into the twentieth century the profession carried a faint whiff of scandal, especially for women. It's not hard to understand why. Acting, after all, is a form of deception, and an actor is a chameleon who can appear to be a king one day and a brain surgeon the next. You never know where you are with actors.

But I have always envied the profession because actors seem so much more lifelike than ordinary mortals, and much better at performing themselves. Actors are better looking, better dressed, better spoken, and more elegant in their movements than the rest of us. Shakespeare said, truthfully enough, that "All the world's a stage, and all the men and women merely players." But how can we amateurs compete with no training, no script and no direction?

The envy and admiration of actors seems to be almost universal. A few were already famous in back the 1800s, but only in the twentieth century, with the arrival of movies, did they become superhuman. The tiny figure on a distant stage suddenly became a demigod on a movie screen twenty feet high, with an amplified voice to match. With special effects he or she could do anything and be anywhere, even on other planets. No wonder so many dreamed about being movie stars, and why the stars themselves became objects of fantasy and worship.

Now everyone can be a star. Streaming services like Netflix, producing new shows at breakneck speed, have created a huge demand for actors, good or bad. Those who can't act at all are put into reality shows.

You don't even need a studio contract or a theater. Technology has provided a personal digital spotlight for us all. We can all have our own little stage and our own little screen, even if it's only a few inches square. Almost everyone I meet under the age of thirty seems to be a singer songwriter or an Internet star with twenty million followers. If you can't act or sing you can become a celebrity by performing home repair or diet therapy on You Tube. It's proof of the universal desire to perform, which we see in children and even in some animals. We are born looking for a stage.

I have always wondered how deeply actors identify with the parts they play. Does Hugh Bonneville really want to be the Earl of Grantham in Downton Abbey? He does it so well. Would Mark Hamill prefer to be Luke Skywalker? Would Diana Rigg like to be the Queen of Thorns? They must believe in their roles to come extent, but to what extent?

Sam Goldwyn used to say: "The most important thing in acting is honesty. Once you can fake that, you've got it made." This reminds us that the biggest and most rewarding stage of all is politics, which these days is pure theater. We will see a great deal of bad political acting in the closing months of 2020, which is fine. It's all part of the universal show. We don't have to believe in it any more than we believe in Game of Thrones. The only worrying thing is that some political actors, dazzled by the lights and the cameras, might begin to believe in their own script and try to *become* the character they play or, worse still, the character they so desperately *want* to play.

First broadcast: January 13, 2020

My Little Shop

As a child I had a rich fantasy life—too rich, I was often told. But my fantasies were important to me, especially the ones about what I would do or be if and when I grew up, which I was in a great hurry to do. In retrospect I can't remember ever wanting to be a train driver or an astronaut or Superman. The fantasy I remember best is the dream of having a little shop. It sounds unlikely now, but it wasn't then.

My dream of becoming a small shopkeeper must have been inspired by weekly shopping trips with my mother to our local high street, which had about twenty establishments. Each shop had a proprietor behind the counter, very much in charge and very much interested in pleasing the customers. We knew their names, and they knew ours. They kept humane and sensible opening hours, closing for two half days each week and all day on Sundays. There were big shiny stores in the city with famous names, like Selfridge's and Harrods, but I had no interest in owning one of them. What I wanted was a little shop. The word "little" was important.

Being a shopkeeper seemed to me like an ideal life. You worked indoors out of the rain, you were your own boss in your own place, you could choose what to sell, and people would just walk in and give you money. I was never interested in becoming a butcher or a baker or a shoe salesman, that was too ordinary. My shop would sell something irresistible like toys or magic tricks or bicycles. Most often, I dreamed about a plain old junk shop, dark and cluttered and smelling of ancient dust. I have a lifelong affinity with junk shops. There was a fine one in our High Street and my mother always tried to keep me out of it. It was jammed to the ceiling with a thousand treasures, broken pieces of machinery, useless tools, dead radios, unstrung guitars, stuffed animals, dog leashes, umbrellas and walking sticks. In those post-war years a lot of military surplus material found its way there too, so I could browse heaps of old two-way radios, electrical testing meters, and cathode ray tubes. It was—the cliché is unavoidable—an Aladdin's Cave of projects and challenges for an inquisitive boy, and I rarely came out without some small treasure costing a few pennies.

Twenty years after those walks along the high street with my mother I had a little shop of my own, a one-room bookstore. I loved it, but not as much as I had expected. Those short hours don't seem so short if you have to be there and stand on your feet the whole time. I learned about stock control, unreliable suppliers, accounting, shoplifting, and difficult customers. There are plenty of those in a bookshop. People go to the butcher for a nice lamb chop or some ground beef, and then they leave. But they go to a bookshop in search of something they heard about, something magical, ineffable, life changing. But of course they have forgotten both the author and the title. A bookseller needs a lot of patience.

I should have stayed with my original dream: a nice junk shop full of stuff that nobody wanted, where no demanding customer would ever come to disturb my tranquility. It could have been the career of a lifetime.

First broadcast: January 27, 2020

Self-esteem for All

February is International Self-Esteem Month, when we are encouraged to boost our morale, and to inspire ourselves and others to seize new challenges. Unfortunately I haven't caught up with the old challenges yet, and I don't think that my morale needs boosting. I have just exactly as much morale as I need to get through the day, and not an iota more.

If there is one thing in the world that we don't need more of, it's self-esteem. The daily news is full of politicians and entertainers who are inflated to the point of exploding with self-esteem. It is not just annoying, it is also potentially dangerous. That's why we have many negative words to describe it: pride (one of the seven deadly sins); egotism; narcissism; smugness; conceit; vanity; vainglory; and of course *hubris*. They all lead to trouble because they are all based on false information. Self-esteem is always a mistake.

We hear a lot about the problem of young people who lack self-esteem. But, if they have done nothing and achieved nothing, their low self-esteem is completely appropriate. In any case they keep it well hidden. The young people I meet seem to assume that they are the masters of the universe. They have been fed on false self-esteem like candy from an early age, and they have forgotten or were never told that it had to be justified somehow, some time.

The ghost of Sigmund Freud hovers over this debate. Nobody likes Freud anymore because his theories challenge our current prejudices. He made a distinction between self-esteem and self-control, which he called the ego and the superego. A correspondent in *The New York Times*, P. M. Formi, expressed the distinction rather well: "Excessive self-esteem is a sort of drunkenness of the self. Self-control is our inner designated driver."

What we need is an objective measure of self-esteem so that we could have it checked, like blood pressure. Zero would represent too much humility and self-doubt and a hundred would indicate a dangerous level of monomania, right up there in the autocratic/dictatorial range. The doctor would check our reading and say: "Self-esteem's a bit too high today, you've been admiring yourself again. Go out and do something embarrassing." The doctor knows that a reasonable dose of humiliation every day is necessary to keep the ego in balance.

Eventually, we may discover a medication for persistent high self-esteem, just as we have for high blood pressure. Meanwhile here are some emergency measures. You can always get some perspective on yourself from the Hubble space telescope, which has revealed fifty billion more galaxies out there, each one of which contain hundreds of millions of stars, and is hundreds of millions of light years across, which is more than the entire length of the New Jersey Turnpike. If the contemplation of that doesn't put you in your place, try reading a college physics textbook, or *The Idiots Guide to Windows 10*. If even this fails, get some cats. You can't have both self-esteem and cats.

We don't continue to celebrate President's Day or Halloween or Thanksgiving long after the date has passed. So we can quickly forget about International Self-Esteem Month. From March to January we can all get real.

First broadcast: February 3, 2020

The Virus That Would Not Go Away

Reflections on COVID-19

Alone Together at Last

I have been known to complain bitterly about computers and the Internet, even as I use them every day. In fact I complain every day, starting when I switch the machine on. But it occurs to me in the present strange situation that I may have been wrong, that computers are leading us towards a new, safer and more survivable world.

The very essence of the Internet is physical separation. It puts distance between one human being and another. You can chat to your friends and family, perhaps for years, without ever having to see them, touch them, or smell them. You can remotely watch your children sleeping in their beds or your aged parents sleeping in their nursing home. Automated checkouts are everywhere so you don't have to speak to a fellow human, or you can order your food and just about everything else online, so you don't have to go out at all. At the bank your friendly tellers are being replaced by machines that look like cheap props left over from a Star Wars movie. Soon the Uber that comes to your door will have nobody in the driving seat, and remote diagnosis is gaining ground in medical practice. Remote treatment, remote surgery, and remote funerals cannot be far behind.

As for the schools and universities, distance learning is already well established and will soon be universal, so a great many unsightly buildings can be demolished, and a great many ugly yellow buses sent to the junkyard. This will be a huge bonus for young people, enormously increasing their leisure time. As a kid I hated going to school, and always wanted to put as much distance between myself and my teachers as possible. Even if distance learning doesn't work very well, ignorance will be no handicap because smart machines will soon do everything for us.

Most of our person-to-person contacts are becoming unnecessary. Social media offer an unlimited source of imaginary friends. Television and computers bring any amount of entertainment into the home, including virtual sports for those athletically inclined. The intimate rituals of love and courtship have been simplified and speeded up on the Internet. Nobody has quite solved the problem of babies yet, but they will. Face to face meetings and conferences were always a complete waste of time and money, and can now be relegated to cyberspace.

The caring guardians of the state will find it much easier to keep their many eyes on us without using intrusive human spies or secret police. CCTV cameras will monitor where we go, and super computers will keep track of our phone calls and e-mails. Wars can be safely conducted from hygienic bunkers, using drones, while peaceful drones can deliver our packages.

This is all very encouraging. The virus scare is pushing us swiftly towards the kind of society that we obviously want and need—an effortless electronic utopia of isolated individuals, each in his or her own pod with his or her own screen. This is truly the right technology at the right time.

The only problem is money. I mean real money, cash, not electronic money which is an illusion invented by the financial industry. Coins and notes are inevitably and necessarily contaminated, and they pass continuously from hand to hand with no thought of hygiene whatsoever. But that is about to change. We are on the verge a cashless economy in which we will spend our imaginary electronic money, all alone with our contactless credit cards, and no virus will stand a chance.

First broadcast: March 23, 2020

Quarantine Memories

Viruses have been a plague on the human race forever. The common cold is the most familiar of them all, but even a cold can be deadly. Beethoven caught a cold when he was going to visit his mother on a freezing winter night, and died. But there are at least five thousand more of these aggravating little monsters and, as we've seen, they keep changing and improving their ability to cause trouble.

I can claim that I once played a tiny part in the eternal battle against viruses. Fifty years ago, as an impoverished graduate student, I spent two weeks as a paid volunteer at an establishment called The Cold Research Center near Salisbury in England. It was a perfect getaway, because we were human guinea pigs held in complete isolation for the duration of the experiments. They tested whether we could catch the virus by being wet or chilled, by sitting in a draft, or even by having the live viruses inserted into our noses.

To protect the integrity of the experiment and the health of everyone else we were quarantined in old army huts in the middle of a vast, empty plain. The accommodation was simple, and there was nothing so luxurious as a television, or even a radio. The memory of those isolated weeks set me thinking about our present situation, and how we can make the most of it.

It could be seen as a preview of the leisure society we've been hearing about for so long. What do we do when we have nothing to do? Quarantine is a challenge and an opportunity. We can't do much to improve the body indoors, although gentle exercises like Tai Chi or Pilates couldn't do too much harm. But this gift of quiet time might allow us to improve the *mind*. I hope you remembered to stock up with books as well as toilet rolls, because the libraries are closed and books are essential. This is a wonderful self-educational opportunity. We can catch up with the latest novels, learn a new language or to dive into some scientific or historical field that we never had time to explore before. There are thousands of online courses and, for relaxation, an unlimited supply of beautiful music, on Public Radio of course.

If improving your mind doesn't appeal to you there is always daytime TV, which will have exactly the opposite effect. And there is always sleep. Statistics tell us that 35% of Americans don't get nearly enough sleep. Here's our chance.

My own long-ago encounter with quarantine stays in my memory as a time of great peacefulness, when I slept a lot and read a whole heap of books with no distractions. I survived the tests and treatments without so much as a sneeze, and left my solitary confinement at the Research Center rather proud of my part in this great humanitarian medical enterprise. Immediately after leaving I caught a terrible cold from somebody on the train.

That's the way it is with virus research. It's a game of scientific hide and seek that never seems to end. My personal contribution to the research was negligible. There are as many common colds as there ever were, and more viruses of every kind. But I have no desire to volunteer as a guinea pig for the latest novel virus. My days as a guinea pig are over. I'm staying home to improve my mind.

First broadcast: March 30, 2020

The Literary Hermit

Every year, immediately after Memorial Day, we are bombarded with lists of recommended summer vacation reading, some of which are so long and so daunting that nervous people may choose not to go on vacation at all. But, in 2020, Memorial Day had nothing to do with it. We needed something good to read right then, in this strange enforced vacation period.

Summer reading is for the beach, but quarantine reading is for the apartment or the suburban house, which is a very different place psychologically. It seems to me that the best strategy is to blend the themes of our quarantine reading into the themes of our peculiar situation in a positive way. Medical books must be avoided at all costs of course, along with the classic plague stories of Albert Camus and Daniel Defoe. These are educational and horrifying, and not the right thing at all.

Reading choices are personal, so I won't even attempt to suggest what *you* should read during your virus vacation. But I can tell you what I've been reading so far.

My luckiest choice was a long novel, *A Gentleman in Moscow* by an author who should be better known, Amor Towles. It is the deceptively simple story is of an aristocratic Russian gentleman, Count Rostov, who in 1922, after the communist revolution, is arrested by the

Bolsheviks and put under house arrest in a small room in a Moscow hotel. He is never allowed to leave the hotel and lives there for over thirty years, never lonely, never depressed or self-pitying about his imprisonment, always making the most of his small world and the people in it, and always well-mannered, always kind. He is no saint, this aristocrat, but he is a genius in the art of making the most of a bad situation. *A Gentleman in Moscow* kept me happy and contented for two weeks.

Crime stories are always a good distraction. Many of the best mystery plots involve a closed room or an isolated group, so you can get you imagination to work on the possibilities in real time. P.D. James is the queen of them all, and I am a great fan of Georges Simenon, but there are thousands of others. There's nothing wrong with a good adventure story when you can't adventure much yourself. Captain Aubrey, the hero of Patrick O'Brian's magnificent Napoleonic wars series, ranges the high seas for seventeen volumes, suffering many things much worse than the annoying virus. Long series of books like O'Brian's, or like Trollope's very different Palliser novels, are perfect for this situation. But Marcel Proust's great biographical novel, *In Search of Lost Time*, might be too much. It will get you through this virus and the next, but Proust for the inexperienced reader is like a marathon for the inexperienced runner. You want to tell people that you did it, but you don't want to actually do it.

On the lighter side, don't despise the classic children's books. *Alice in Wonderland*, a festival of human foolishness in a thin disguise, always rewards an adult re-reading, as does *Wind in the Willows* where you learn much about creatures like moles, water rats and toads enjoying life in their natural habitat. Like Count Rostov, the animals in classic children's books, from Winnie-the Pooh to Paddington Bear, always rise above their situation, whatever it is, which is why we love and admire them so much.

First broadcast: April 6, 2020

Saving the Planet

Back in the 1970s, when Earth Day began, it was easy to know what we should do: plant a tree, raise consciousness, promote cleaner air and water. It was a ritual of purification and celebration, a day for us to show how concerned we were about the deterioration of our environment, and our naïve conviction that we could somehow put things right. But none of us wanted to do what really needed to be done: to completely change our way of life.

Fifty years later we can sit back and relax. Our lives are being changed for us. The coronavirus has accomplished what half a century of ecological education and propaganda have failed to accomplish. Our habits have been rearranged exactly as they should be, from an ecological point of view. Don't forget that the greatest global threat is overpopulation. With social distancing discouraging intimacy, the birth rate will certainly fall. As a bonus trillions of gallons of water in unnecessary showers will be saved, along with unimaginable quantities of deodorants and grooming products.

The most striking evidence of our changed lifestyle comes from the maps of global air pollution taken from space. The great dark clouds of smog over the big cities have thinned out and, in some cases, almost faded away. People in Beijing and Delhi could breathe again—through a mask of course, but that was a small price to pay.

This miracle was accomplished in an amazingly short time partly because tourism stopped, and a lot of routine driving stopped. The airlines went into hibernation and the highways were almost empty. The gas tank I filled in Memorial Day lasted almost until Labor Day.

Along with the decrease in pollution came a decrease in consumption. There was still online shopping of course, but casual daily shopping vanished because the stores were closed. In effect, we had rationing. It reminded me of my childhood in England, where rationing began in 1940. It didn't affect me much at first because I wasn't eating solid food at the time. But while I was growing up during and after the war strict rationing was in effect, and continued until 1954. It seemed natural to me that my mother never went anywhere without a bunch of ration books containing coupons, and stood in line for the small weekly allowance. Sometimes the ration was a mere illusion, because the shops were sold out.

Everything was rationed, including gasoline and clothes, and even then there were shortages of toilet paper, so that the sales of cheap tabloid newspapers went up spectacularly. Suburban backyards turned into tiny farms where almost everyone kept chickens, and a lively barter economy emerged. The rich, as usual, paid no attention to rationing and got what they wanted on the black market.

I am tempted to say "It didn't do me any harm," and I don't think it did. We were all right, once the *Luftwaffe* stopped dropping bombs on us, and I think we were even happy. My parents managed with great ingenuity, and with the help of the chickens. Now, as we move forward to the past and navigate this new landscape of restrictions and shortages, we are reliving history without having to watch the History Channel, and, as a bonus, we are helping to save the planet at the same time. It just goes to show—there's always a bright side.

First broadcast: April 20, 2020

A Symbolic Moment

During the week leading up to Easter and Passover a house in our neighborhood had an eye-catching seasonal display. A line of extra-large colored eggs came tumbling down the sloping front lawn, presided over by a big, cheerful bunny. They made me smile every time I passed. Of course I know that bunnies and eggs have nothing to do with Easter or Passover, or at least nothing we are supposed to mention. They are charming echoes of a different and much more ancient tradition, the celebration of spring, which may be as old as humanity. In other words they are fertility symbols.

I had to discover this for myself. My mother never told me. But it is a striking example of how powerful symbols can be, and how they outlast their original meaning and become appropriated for quite different purposes. The Nazi Swastika was originally a symbol of the sun or of divinity in eastern religions, and in the early twentieth century it was the logo on a brand of cheap cigarettes. Symbols are slippery.

Written language began not with alphabets but with symbols like Egyptian hieroglyphs. These ancient picture languages are quite simple—a pot shape represents a pot, a sheaf of wheat represents a sheaf of wheat, and so on. When we are very young and still recapitulating the history of the human race in the laborious process of growing up, we start by drawing things in that primitive style, very simply. A house is not a line of meaningless letters—H-O-U-S-E—it is a little square with a pitched roof, a door, and a chimney emitting a stream of smoke in defiance of environmental regulations. We don't know any better. Eventually we grow up and discover spelling and central heating, but that childish symbol keeps its primordial power, and its charm.

Some symbols function almost as a universal language. Everybody understands the signs for "No Smoking" or "No Entry," and everybody except the French understands a speed limit sign. Other symbols are more like a secret code, for example the mysterious icons on your computer desktop which might mean anything, but usually mean trouble. We also find on our screens little pictures called emoticons to express feelings that, in more literate times, everyone knew how to express in words.

Some symbols were deliberately designed to create solidarity and commitment: national flags religious icons, and the logos of sports teams. Corporations love to invent symbols for themselves, and they too may become virtually part of the language, like the yellow Shell or the three-pointed Mercedes star.

A symbol is a short cut to our feelings, bypassing the process of thought entirely. In the late nineteenth century an artistic and literary movement called symbolism promoted the idea that art need not portray real things but should only symbolize their effects, good or bad. For example the golden arches are not a burger themselves, but they have the *effect* of making you swerve into the drive-through. The Symbolists have long since vanished, but their direct descendants in advertising and politics are everywhere, promoting their simple emotive symbols in place of a more complicated reality.

The symbol of 2020 was to be the sinister, doom-laden image of the Coronavirus seen through a microscope, and millions were hypnotized by it. But symbols are a matter of choice, and for myself I prefer to contemplate the cheerful Easter bunnies and their colored eggs, the ancient symbols of a new beginning.

First broadcast: April 13, 2020

Build We Must

Just about everything came to a standstill during the Coronavirus panic except building. There were active constructions sites all over the place, one of them virtually in our backyard. A big house was being shoehorned into the small space where the last remaining patch of woodland used to be. Under the present administration, the last industry to be closed down would be real estate development.

There was something touchingly optimistic about this suburban building in the midst of the pandemic. It suggested the confident anticipation of willing buyers with mortgages, and money to spare for furniture and home appliances, alarm systems, and all the other things necessary to turn an empty patch of land into a profitable real estate deal. Builders, like tree farmers, must gamble on the long-term future.

There is never much variation in the design of these new homes. You see the same architecture all over Long Island, Connecticut, New Jersey, and much of America. It's as if, in the great suburban explosion of the 1950s and 1960s, the developers set out from the boroughs with half a dozen standard plans, and never felt the need to replace them—Cape, Colonial, Ranch, Victorian and so on over and over again. The few genuine old houses show how little has changed. It seems that we have arrived at the perfect design and need never think about our suburban lifestyle ever again. You can walk into almost any one of these houses and feel at home straight away

It must also make building easier. I observed the construction crew right in front of my window with fascination. They never seemed to consult a plan, either on paper or on a computer. After years of building the same house it was obviously automatic for them, like doing the same jigsaw puzzle over and over. Much of the house arrived like Lego in ready cut pieces ready to fit together.

I was once seriously addicted to a program called This Old House on Public Television. This gave me the chance to see men (and at least one woman) doing the real, hard work of house building. All that TV watching made quite me a knowledgeable critic. Had they got the window insulation just right? Was the flashing around that chimney fixed down tightly enough? The work went slowly because the same crew was building other identical houses in the neighborhood, so I had many weeks of enjoyable backseat building.

Some of these workers were risk-takers, like their employers, and I hope they are paid accordingly. The roofers especially kept me on the edge of my seat. It was a tall house, and they were running around twenty-five feet in the air, carrying heavy nail guns, without any safety equipment that I could see, let alone masks. I suppose they were protected from viruses by social distance of the vertical kind. Nobody was going to climb up there and sneeze on them.

We need our suburban houses of course. We are living in one. For a long time we were virtually hiding in it. After a few weeks of lockdown we were as tightly adapted to our house as a snail to her shell or a hermit to his cave. Thank goodness the design is perfect. We may never want to go out ever again.

First broadcast: April 27, 2020

Kindness to Animals Week

National Be Kind to Animals Week comes around once a year at the beginning of May. This event was created by the Humane Society in 1915 when kindness was in short supply. We seem to be doing better now, but our attitudes to animals are still seriously mixed up.

Some domestic pets have had a hard time in this epidemic. Their routines were changed, dog walks were curtailed, and cats have had to eat inferior food when their own favorite brand ran out. In the worst cases their companionate people fell victim to the virus.

Many communities and organizations mobilized to take care of these distressed pets, which makes you feel better about the human race. Kindness to animals is a measure of civilization, and in some ways it is an easy virtue to practice. We can be kind to animals by recognizing them as fellow creatures and talking to them. Everybody talks to their own pets, and it has a deep psychological effect. The animal "it" becomes a fellow-creature with feelings, and we feel quite differently about our relationship.

I will happily talk to fellow creatures of any kind. The squirrels, chipmunks and deer who cross my path always get a polite word, and they appreciate it I'm sure. The more intelligent animals are, the better they understand human communication. Chipmunks, for example, are rather skittish, unrewarding company, cats are always argumentative, and dogs are rather too apt to agree with every word you say. But you can have a very good conversation with a pig. Winston Churchill had a special fondness for pigs. "Dogs look up to us," he said, "cats look down on us, but pigs treat us as equals."

I caught myself chatting to a pig once, just a couple of hours after having had bacon and eggs for breakfast, and there's the huge contradiction. What sense does it make to be kind to animals in small ways when we treat them abominably in big ways? Talking to pigs and being nice to lost puppies and fluffy kittens is obviously not enough, and never will be enough until we all turn vegetarian or vegan, which I, along with most of the human race, have disgracefully failed to do.

In the COVID-19 year a whole other level of animal exploitation was forced on our attention. The nasty new virus seems to have originated in China's notorious "wet markets" where live animals are caged and sold for use in traditional medicine, otherwise known as medieval quackery. The beautiful Pangolin for example is used to treat, among other things, anxiety and deafness. You are as likely to be cured of deafness by eating the scales of the Pangolin as you are to be cured of the Coronavirus by swallowing disinfectant. It is magical thinking, profoundly irrational and dangerous. The animals suffer, and so do we.

We've come a long way since the first Be Kind to Animals week 1915. But, let's face it, we have brought the present calamity on ourselves by cruelty and indifference, and not just in China. Kindness to animals is not a charity or a weakness, it is simple self-interest. We share the same biosphere, and many of the same bacteria and viruses, as well as the same feelings. We're all connected. The more kind we are to them, the more kind we are to ourselves.

First broadcast: May 4, 2020

Bored in the USA

For some of us at least the long-awaited leisure society seems to have arrived at last. But time moves slowly when we have nothing to do, and the threat of boredom is always just around the corner. The highlights of our week may be a visit from the UPS van, a Skype call, or a plumbing emergency when there are no plumbers. Small animal events outside the window—a passing deer, a hawk, or an acrobatic squirrel—have become incredibly interesting. There's nothing new to talk about except the one subject we want to avoid. We are tired of our own books and DVDs, television is nothing but violence and perpetual Antiques Road Show repeats, while the streaming services are apparently designed for creatures from some other planet. Life has become nothing but reruns and repetitions.

Our problem is that we have lost the gift of idleness, and it may be time to claim it back. People have been wondering how to deal with idleness for a long time, probably since the beginning of time. A wet Sunday afternoon in the Paleolithic era before the invention of books must have been incredibly boring. My favorite character in literature, Oblomov, dealt with it by refusing to leave his bed. The great polymath Dr. Samuel Johnson published over a hundred essays under the general title of "The Idler" on topics of no importance whatsoever such as marriage announcements, shopping for bargains, and how to succeed in doing nothing. A new version of The Idler magazine was founded 1993 dedicated to the art of living pointlessly. I found an old copy around the house (I can't imagine why) which has inspiring articles on paper airplanes, smoking in the bath, and being an incompetent bird watcher. The same team presides over the Idler Academy of Philosophy, Husbandry and Merriment, offering such courses as sourdough bread baking and ukulele playing. These idleness experts seem to tell us that the secret of empty time is to fill it up with sleep or futile amusements. This is how children get through childhood, before the days of their lives are claimed by jobs, families, and overdue bills.

In 1932 the British philosopher and pacifist Bertrand Russell published a provocative essay called "In Praise of Idleness." His main argument was that idleness tends to promote peace, whereas restless, anxious, competitive activity tends to promote war. This makes perfect sense. Wars, after all, are hard work. A truly idle nation would be a peaceful nation.

Russell conceded that some work was necessary and useful for society, so that everybody (and he meant *everybody*, not just the poor) should work for about four hours a day. A huge leisure class would be created and everyone would be free, in Russell's phrase, to follow his or her curiosity. He didn't approve of futile amusements. He proposed we should all pursue and develop our intellectual, artistic and creative interests, whatever they are. The result would be a much happier and more stimulating society, economically poorer but culturally much richer. He even argued that, without the exhaustion caused by too much work, we could abandon our passive and mindless entertainments. In short, we would all become smarter.

Following Bertrand Russell's advice I could use my empty time to take up some worthwhile and absorbing project that will keep me busy and mentally challenged for months, if not years. I could learn a difficult language, or try harder to understand quantum mechanics, or take up the violin. On the other hand, somewhere around the house, I know, we have a big, unfinished jigsaw puzzle.

First broadcast: May 11, 2020

Tough Guys

We all know how difficult adolescent boys can be especially if, like me, you had the unfortunate experience of being one. The adolescent male attitude seems to be built into our DNA, like a set of rules for annoying behavior. Never explain, never apologize, never admit a mistake, never show sympathy, let alone empathy, never admit that you care about anything except sports, never listen to reason, and never hear any inconvenient facts.

We have all been there, or at least the male half of the population has been there. Adolescent girls, of course, are perfect in every way, or that's what I've been told. This unpleasant masculine life stage is probably a necessary rite of passage for young men who are trying to separate emotionally from their mothers and be accepted as real men by their own age group. It is certainly irritating, but entirely natural and probably served a purpose in more primitive societies when mindless male aggression and toughness was an essential survival mechanism. In prehistoric times nice guys didn't just finish last, they never finished at all.

I admired tough guys when I was young. All the best movies for kids came from America in those days, and we loved to see the cowboys perpetually shooting each other for no particular reason, the GIs winning the war with overwhelming firepower, and fearless policemen and detectives serving out justice in a hail of bullets, to say nothing of superheroes who destroyed just about everything and everybody in sight. Good and bad, they were all tough guys, and the movies offered a world perfectly designed for dimwitted young boys to live in, with never a thought or even a hint that humanity had progressed beyond the Paleolithic Age. It was just about the only model of masculinity on offer for the pre-baby boom generation, and it had the advantage of being easy to understand. All you had to do to be tough was to put your invincible self at the center of the universe, despise everybody else, and always be ready for a fight.

Most of us left that childish fantasy behind, although it was fun while it lasted. Once common sense has dawned, we feel no need to pretend to be tough guys. It *is* virtually all pretense, and what I call the white collar tough guy is usually just faking it, and would run away from any physical threat. Life is too short and too complicated for all that macho playacting, and at some point most of us gave up the game. This process is called growing up.

Growing up is not as popular as it used to be. The COVID-19 epidemic revealed not only the real toughness of first responders and frontline medical staffs, but also the fake toughness of a lot of prominent men who seem to have reverted to adolescence. The almost pathological lack of empathy in the Trump administration was clearly related to their self-image as tough guys.

They perfected the sour, hostile, swaggering adolescent pose, a toxic mixture of fear and aggression. We see it on our TV screens all the time, and it's a sad spectacle to see men in their sixties and seventies wearing expensive suits but still acting like resentful teenagers, refusing to take responsibility, throwing out insults, and taking sides as if this was a game.

But this is no time for games. It's time to grow up.

First broadcast: May 18, 2020

Travel Interrupted

Memorial Day is the traditional start of the summer season with its vacations, festivals, barbecues foreign travels, and long lazy days at the beach. But not in 2020.

When the curtain came down on foreign travel we were packed and ready to leave for Europe. Flights, trains and hotel bookings were all in order. But needless to say we went nowhere. We tried to create a shadow version of our European summer on Long Island, sitting on the terrace wearing shorts and straw hats and drinking French wine. The scenery was not what we could have wished, but it was the most economical vacation we ever had.

The question in your mind, and mine, is: can the deprivation of luxuries really be described as a deprivation? How much are we really suffering if we can't go to a concert, or if the supermarket delivers the wrong kind of cheese? The answer is, not much. "Everything is relative" is one of the emptiest platitudes in the English language. Everything is *not* relative, especially not now. A few cancelled airline tickets scarcely weigh in the balance against what a great many people have had to endure.

We can squeeze a grain of satisfaction from the environmental bonus. Flights are down by ninety per-cent, driving by fifty per-cent, and we've all seen the dramatic pictures that show how air pollution has been reduced as a result. The lesson is obvious. We should stop travelling huge distances at great expense for trivial reasons: to sit on a particular beach, ski down a particular slope or indulge in a particular cuisine. If we all stopped doing those things the world would change, indeed it has changed. The citizens of Venice can walk around freely in their own city, Rome and Paris are empty, and the most popular tourist destinations can literally breathe again.

The only small problem is that tourism is or was one of the world's biggest industries, worth about nine trillion dollars to the global economy. Nothing is more human than the desire to be somewhere else. The idea of being stuck always in the same place, a kind of permanent global lockdown, is intolerable. So, little by little, cautiously, we will start buying air tickets again and, if history is any guide, we will soon be behaving exactly as we were before.

History is very good guide, but only if we remember it. The ancient Greeks believed that history moved in circles because we always forget what happened in the past, especially the bad things, and then make exactly the same mistakes again. Wars are the prime example of this. If we remembered the wars of the past we wouldn't need a Memorial Day, but we do. It is possible that this collective amnesia is a survival mechanism. If we really recalled all the catastrophic events that make our history so interesting we might be paralyzed by anxiety and doubt.

But this time, surely, it's different. .We will remember this, and plan for it, and be ready for it next time. Of course we will.

First broadcast: May 24, 2920

Walls and Masks

One of the earliest human discoveries must have been how to build a defensive wall. Almost immediately afterwards the door was invented so the builders could get out. Archaeologists, looking for traces of ancient human occupation, always look first for signs of stone walls, or wooden palisades, or earthen mounds thrown up to keep those inside safe from those outside. It suggests that we were even less neighborly in prehistoric times than we are now.

Walls have always been popular. In Europe in past centuries every city and town had a wall with guarded gates, which were often difficult for a stranger to pass and were closed at nightfall. When the plague was abroad in medieval Europe, cities threw out all foreigners and locked the gates, because *somebody* had to be blamed for the infection. The citizens meanwhile shut themselves in their houses and wore cloth masks around their faces. So nothing much has changed in public health policy in five hundred years.

You can still see the remains of those city walls in many places, as well as impressive fortresses with walls up to forty feet high, calculated to discourage casual visitors. But none them worked for long. In fact the ruins of walls found all over the world are a testimony to the fact that they were ultimately a huge waste of time and effort.

New York had an impressive wall in the 1600s, designed to keep undesirable people out. It failed. The British soon found a way round it. The site is now called Wall Street, which is a symbolic wall also designed to keep undesirable people out, and it works better. But America never became a nation of walled cities, apart from a few forts out in the Wild West when it was even wilder than it is now. On the contrary cities were wide open and, in the suburbs, great sweeps of suburban lawn ran from one home to another without a break, which always impressed European visitors. Americans seemed to accept that the price of community was openness—literal, physical openness. You could say that the lack of walls and fences was a rough measure of civilization, or at least of trust and self-confidence.

Trust in America is now in short supply, as is the sense of community. We are building walls and gated subdivisions as fast as we can. In an attempt to deal with the Coronavirus disaster we are reduced to hiding behind masks, which are a personal wall against unwanted viruses. Masks, like walls, have a long and complicated history. Executioners wore masks, as did Klansmen, as do surgeons. The masked ball encouraged disguise as part of an elaborate sexual game, and masked crusaders like Zorro pretended that a small strip of black cloth would make them invisible. We all want to be invisible sometimes. We all understand the desire to conceal or be concealed, to isolate or be isolated.

In everyday life a mask is unwelcoming, like a wall, and even threatening. All our normal human signals are concealed and we are reduced to a clumsy form of sign language. And masks, like walls, have taken on multiple political meanings. A wall can say: I'm strong, I can defeat you or I'm scared, I'm hiding. A mask too can send a message of fear or defiance, and it seems that both can be political in a hyper-political atmosphere. Those who like walls don't like masks, and vice versa. Some see walls as sign of strength, and masks as a sign of weakness. In this confused world of tribal fears and fantasies what we need above all is steady, rational, nonpartisan leadership. While we wait for that miracle to happen it might be safer to continue hiding behind your mask.

First broadcast: June 1, 2020

The End of Education?

In 1995 the cultural critic Neil Postman published a book with the provocative title *The End of Education,* arguing that the public school system had fundamentally failed. Others have taken up the same theme over the years. Ivan Illich in *De-Schooling Society* advocated the abolition of schools altogether, and H. L. Mencken, the satirical Baltimore columnist, when asked what should be done to improve public education, said: "Burn the buildings and hang the professors."

None of these proposals has been tried yet, but now we have a massive uncontrolled real-life experiment that may show whether or not there is a better way to educate children than in large bureaucratic institutions. For the moment, for millions of children, school has become home and home has become school.

The transition to home schooling must be difficult. The noble idea of universal education took root in the 1850s, driven by the belief that democracy could not survive without an educated population. Now, as so often happens, the system has grown into a monster with 130,000 schools, more than three million teachers, and uncounted numbers of bureaucrats and administrators.

This system has effectively monopolized education for a hundred and fifty years. How can unaided parents hope to replace it? How many of them are qualified to teach, or have the patience and stamina to cover the whole curriculum? Children have an even bigger adjustment to make. For them, home has been a safe space—safe from things like algebra and vocabulary. They have been accustomed to seeing their parents as loving protectors, and their little electronic screens as nothing but fun. It must be an awful shock when parents and devices start posing nasty mathematical puzzles and quizzes on German verbs, as if Mickey Mouse had turned into Darth Vader.

Home schooling is a lottery. Everything depends on the home. Many children are unlucky enough to have parents who are ignorant, or religious fanatics, or abusers. School is a refuge for such children, and being stuck at home is a catastrophe. This is the best argument for those who say: "Back to school at any price." But it shouldn't lead us to forget the essential difference between schooling and education.

The purpose of schooling, is to pass on a toolkit of useful knowledge and techniques that will allow children to get along in this complicated world. Their parents can scarcely be expected to do this. Most moms and dads are smart enough to stay a chapter ahead in the textbook, or check out a computer lesson in advance. But the range of knowledge to be taught is just too vast, and teaching it is a specialized skill. Schooling, in this sense, will have to wait a while until a new system emerges, or until we go back to the old system.

What children need right now to fill the gap in their lives is not home schooling but home education. Education was happening at home long before schools were invented, and its purpose was to bring children up with some appreciation of what we might call Civilization 101—

old-fashioned qualities like morality, curiosity, self-control, and emotional literacy. Education is about growing up and becoming a decent human being. No large buildings or yellow buses are necessary. This is what parents have always done. Unlike professional teachers they are not suffocated by bureaucracy or harassed by mandatory paperwork and tests. Not all parents are doctors of philosophy or bachelors of education, but they have all been educated in life, and by life, and have made the usual mistakes. They can teach what they know, and they will find that they know a lot.

Let parents take care of the education, and schooling will eventually take care of itself.

First broadcast: June 8, 2020

Bloomsday Unmasked

One of my quarantine projects has been to catch up with my reading, and now I have an unread book on my mind, a splendid and impossible book: *Ulysses* by James Joyce. But why now? Because every year in the middle of June, and uniquely in literature, this book has a special commemorative day known as "Bloomsday."

If you are not an English major you may need a footnote here. Bloomsday is observed every June 16 in Dublin, Ireland, to commemorate the life of James Joyce and to relive the events in his novel *Ulysses*, all of which took place on the same day in Dublin in 1904. There are public readings and dramatizations from the book, guided walks around Dublin, and frequent stops at the historic pubs.

Things are less simple when you try to read the book itself, which is seven hundred and eighty three pages long, including footnotes. The main character in the novel is Leopold Bloom, hence the title, and June 16 was the date of Joyce's own first walk with his future wife. The novel loosely follows the adventures of Ulysses from Homer's *Odyssey*. The characters represent those in Homer's epic, with Leopold Bloom cast as Ulysses. The characters explore various sites and happenings around Dublin such as a newspaper office, a brothel, a funeral, and public houses. Beyond this, the book is indescribable. Nothing is made easy for the reader. Joyce changes the order of events in the original story, uses stream of consciousness and other 'modernist' techniques, invents brand new words, and includes hundreds of obscure references. This is a novel that you have to read with several academic commentaries to hand, and indeed there are reading groups, clubs, and web networks whose members do nothing but slog through the pages of *Ulysses*. It's a lifetime commitment.

I took my first shot at reading *Ulysses* back in the sixties, when I thought I wanted to be an intellectual. I read as far as lunchtime on June 16, when Leopold Bloom visits the National Museum in Dublin, before deciding that being an intellectual just wasn't worth it. A few years later I tried again, this time reading backwards from the end in the hope that the book would reveal its secret that way. No luck. Once a year I pick *Ulysses* off the shelf, where it takes up a lot of space, turning it this way and that, like a Rubik Cube, trying to grasp the reason for its extraordinary fame and influence. It's amazingly *clever*, I can see that. But that's all I can see, which no doubt is my problem.

A book so formidable may be worth the effort, no matter what it costs or how long it takes, because you would get such a sense of satisfaction just from having read it. It would be one of those lifetime achievements to brag about, like climbing Everest or reading the whole of Proust's *Remembrance of Things Past* in French. I have done only one of those.

But is there any *virtue* in reading such a book? Does it tune up the brain, like Mozart's music or *The Times* crossword? Or can it, as I rather suspect, bring on the mental equivalent of a computer crash? Black screen, fatal error.

Ireland has suffered as much from the Coronavirus as anywhere else, and is still in recovery. So Bloomsday will not be quite the same this year. Here are the new rules for the celebration: *don't* attend the public readings, *don't* walk around Dublin, and *don't,* whatever you do, stop in the historic pubs. It doesn't sound like much fun. The only thing you can do, or try to do on Bloomsday—and, of course this is the hard part—is to stay safely at home and read the book.

First broadcast: June 15, 2020

Beauty and the Beast

My favorite barbershop was closed for three months during the epidemic. On the first day of re-opening I drove past the shop to see if this liberation was real. A crowd of disheveled men waited outside, while in the interior I could see a wild scene of tonsorial activity, with every other chair occupied. This was a great relief. I never had much hair to begin with, but my small crop has flourished mightily and I had assumed the appearance of a hedgehog with curls. For the past three months I had scarcely dared to appear on the radio. Eventually (but not on that first day) I allowed my barber to restore my hair to its natural state, whatever that is. He knows better than I.

A good barbershop is hard to find. When a man needs a haircut he needs just that, a haircut, nothing complicated. An authentic barbershop will display a symbolic candy-striped pole outside, and will be starkly utilitarian inside. Until the eighteenth century barbers also acted as rough-and-ready surgeons at prices far below the current AMA rates. This proud history should be reflected in the plainness of the decor: it should look like an operating theater. Carpets and flowers, pastel colors and hair dryers, are a sure sign that the place is on the downhill slide to becoming a unisex establishment, or even a beauty salon.

The deprivation of hair care has obviously been even harder for women whose needs are more complicated. The closing of beauty salons was deeply unpopular in France, where they are twice as numerous as they are in America, and in Italy where, in June, hair and nail salons opened to a huge rush of business with appointments scheduled months ahead. Plastic surgeons also had a big surge in bookings, so it seems that a few weeks without beauty treatments have prompted some painful decisions.

In the French village where we used to live there was a single barber in the market square. His cramped shop was packed with farmers discussing wine and local politics in the incomprehensible local dialect. His grooming technique was less like that of a hairdresser than of a lawn service. His wildly flying scissors sometimes drew blood *("pardon monsieur")* and I privately named him Sweeney the Barberarian. He left me little choice but to patronize one of the local beauty salons, where I was received kindly although with some surprise. There, in the five minutes it took Muriel to cut my hair, I caught a glimpse of the incredibly complex infrastructure of female hair beauty. I won't give anything away, except that it seems to involve a lot of chemicals and a lot of time. There's nothing more disillusioning than seeing how women get their hair the way they do. It's like taking one of the underground tours in Disney World, where you discover how the above-ground illusions are created.

There is something about hair that touches our deepest obsessions. It is the last vestige of our animal selves, the last scrap of protective fur for our tribe of naked apes. The symbolism is powerful. Samson proverbially lost his muscle tone when he was shorn of his locks. The cutting of hair has been a form of domination at least since Caesar did it to the Gauls in 52 BC. Short hair often indicates submission to a discipline, as in the bullet-headed military cut, or the penitential monastic style. At the other extreme, elaborate and high-maintenance hair styles for men indicate either a narcissistic desire to be looked at, or the absence of a mirror in the bathroom. These differences are symbolically rich and at the same time completely contradictory, which makes them very human. We love symbolism, but we hate it to make sense.

When unisex haircutting first came along it seemed like a blow for sexual equality. Through the ages, women had been handicapped in the race of life not only by male chauvinism but by the demands of hair care. Men of my generation can remember when their dates washed their hair so often and for so long that drowning seemed a distinct possibility. These same unfortunate women would regularly waste whole mornings in the beauty salon, come out looking like a cross between Madonna and Medusa, and pay a small fortune for the privilege. By contrast, a man's haircut was a quick, low-cost affair, over in ten minutes.

In the eighteenth and nineteenth centuries, men's barbershops often had musical instruments on the walls so that clients could entertain themselves while waiting. This must be the origin of the barbershop quartet. The modern barbershop is less lively but still adequately sociable. Instead of musical instruments there's a big screen television showing nothing but sports, and the waiting men stare up at that, or stare down at their phones, hoping for the miracle that everyone seems to expect from the tiny screen. Anyone who dared to play an instrument or sing would probably be asked to leave. But it is a companionable space, quiet except for the buzz of clippers, the insistent voice of the television, and a low mutter of conversation about sports. Nothing bad or embarrassing can happen to a man in a barbershop. It is the closest thing to a private club or a spiritual home that he is likely to find. There's no need to worry about styling because an old-fashioned barber makes no concessions to style. He will ask: "How do you want it cut, sir?" But this is a mere formality. Everyone gets the identical short back and sides which is the perfect male fashion statement, an unmistakable badge of ordinariness and modesty. The addition of a baseball cap makes it just about perfect.

First broadcast: June 22, 2020

Walking Alone

The COVID-19 scare has changed the landscape of exercise. Walking has become the national hobby, although this probably won't outlast the epidemic. The gym crowd will go back to their sweaty machines the moment they can, and all the other newly-dedicated walkers will vanish like morning mist when the weather gets colder. But, in the summer of 2020, there were so many walkers of all ages that it was hard to keep a proper social distance from them.

Walking has been deeply unfashionable in America ever since the invention of the motor car. Foreign visitors have frequently observed that this is a nation dedicated not to equality, as the Declaration of Independence claims, but to inactivity. People will go to great lengths to avoid walking even a few steps. Comical contests take place in supermarket car parks to decide who will park their cars (equipped with every energy-saving device) closest to the door in order to save the exertion of walking fifty feet. Food delivery has abolished this problem.

There are practical reasons for this aversion to walking. It can be dangerous. The unsteady vertical arrangement of our bodies on two legs means that we are always on the edge of falling, and it gets worse as we get older. As George Orwell put it in *Animal Farm*, Four legs good, two legs bad.

But, with practice, walking can be safely attempted even for several hundred yards at a time.

After what seemed like a long time crawling around on the floor I learned to walk at the age of about fourteen months, and I've been walking ever since. I liked walking from the start. It was more dignified than crawling, and faster, and it allowed me to see more things. Some medical authorities have even suggested that walking may be good for our physical health, although we should probably reserve judgement on that.

There are better reasons to believe that walking is good for our *mental* health, although most of the evidence comes from the past when people used their feet much more than we do now. It may help to explain the astonishing creative and intellectual brilliance of certain characters in history. How did they achieve so much? It certainly wasn't good health care, or even good health. What their biographies show is that many of them walked a lot, not only from necessity but also from choice. Here's a short list to consider.

The peripatetic philosophers of ancient Greece who walked from city to city all over Asia minor, the poets of the Romantic Age like Wordsworth and Blake, the philosopher, Jean Jacques Rousseau, Henry David Thoreau who wrote a book about walking, Ralph Waldo Emerson, Charles Dickens who was reputed to walk twenty miles a day, Robert Louis Stevenson, Virginia Woolf, Vladimir Nabokov, George Orwell himself, the composers Brahms, Beethoven, Tchaikovsky, and Dvorak. The list could be extended almost indefinitely. They were all great walkers.

The mechanical business of walking and the freedom of being outdoors, taken together, seem to expand the mind. There's no competition, no speed, no hurry, no rules, and usually no disturbance. What could be more conducive to creative thinking? That's the secret, I'm sure, of our astonishingly productive ancestors. They walked a great deal, and therefore thought a great deal. The philosopher Nietzsche wrote: "Do not believe any idea that was not born in the open air, and of free movement."

The new walkers of the COVID-19 era tend to some in groups, often family groups or tight little bunches of teenage girls (never boys, for some reason) walking and talking and looking at their phones all at the same time. These groups are rarely masked, perhaps on the assumption that they are safe with each other and therefore safe with everybody, which may prove to be a deadly mistake. Some of them, I assume, are refugees from the closed gyms and fitness centers, and others are escaping from stay-at-home claustrophobia.

The problem about walking in a group is that is cancels one of the main benefits. Walking time is thinking time, and distraction can ruin a good walk. That's why it's important to walk alone sometimes, because the whole walking experience is about being with yourself and thinking about the world around you. The very ground under your feet becomes part of the experience, if only you pay attention, *quietly*. You can't talk and think at the same time, which is why cellphones are so popular and why so many walkers come in pairs or groups, talking every inch of the way.

Enlightenment is not guaranteed. You can take a long peaceful ramble in the country, never meet another person, and come back with your head as empty as before. It happens to me all the time. But then at least I had a nice quiet walk.

First broadcast: June 29, 2020

On the Beach

On the Fourth of July in 2020 the Covid restrictions were lifted and thousands of people rushed to the beach. The seashore is a magnet. Seventy five percent of Americans choose to live within fifty miles of the coast. We are especially lucky on Long Island. Because the island is nothing but a beach, a narrow finger of sand, getting narrower every year. So we are never far from the sea just as we are never far from a pizza place. We scarcely ever *see* the sea, because so much of the shoreline is private property. But it's nice to know that the sea is there for those who can afford it, and that the occasional public beach provides some access to it.

Our family vacations long ago were taken on the beaches of southern England. They call this area the English Riviera, demonstrating the famous British sense of humor. I remember quite vividly the peculiarly nasty texture of wet sand, and our picnics in the car or the bus shelter with the rain pouring down outside. When we did manage to picnic on the beach the food was heavily seasoned with sand and wasps. My sand castles were washed away by the tide or stomped by older children. I was tormented by sinister eels hiding under rocks, stinging jellyfish, freezing waves, sharp stones, clinging, foul-smelling seaweed, folding beach chairs that folded by themselves and trapped your fingers, and boredom.

So I occupied by time by digging deep holes in the sand, hoping that somebody would fall into them in the shadowless blaze of high noon. This was an idea I got from a picture book about prehistoric hunters who persuaded mammoths to fall into their traps. But I never trapped a mammoth or anybody else because there was never any sun at high noon. When I think about having a good time, a beach is not the first place that comes to my mind. I've seen more attractive and even warmer beaches since then, but it may take more than one lifetime to shake off those early impressions. You can't sit or read comfortably on a beach, unless you take your own furniture, and there's nothing much else to do apart from swimming in cold water of unknown cleanliness.

But mine is a minority point of view, rooted in those traumatic childhood experiences, a kind of PBSD or Post Beach Stress Disorder. Beaches are enormously popular with those grew up in friendlier climates. Now that I am much older, and a little wiser, and living in a warmer climate, I understand that my problem with the beach was childish *naivité*. I stopped going to them at exactly the age when I should have started. Beaches aren't for kids. They are sandy stage sets for young adults to show off their young and beautiful bodies, and to admire the aesthetic qualities of other young and beautiful bodies, and to get as close as possible to other young and beautiful bodies. Beaches are the ultimate outdoor mating and dating service, and children are the result rather than the cause of all this fun in the sun.

City dwellers have been escaping to the beach since the overheated citizens of ancient Rome discovered Ostia more than two thousand years ago, and modern Italians rushed back to their beaches the moment they were released from quarantine, they couldn't wait. All through the late summer of 2020 the beaches were packed with people sunbathing and socializing as if they had never heard of COVID-19, or dermatology.

The beach is certainly a great excuse for doing nothing, because there is nothing much you can do. It is a big beautiful sand box where you can take your shoes off, maybe take everything off, and play. It's the meeting place of water, land, humanity and sunshine—a liminal space on the edge of the everyday world, where just about anything goes. Poets like Byron, Shelley, and Swinburne have loved and celebrated this liminal space on the edge of the sea.

So the word "beach" for many people conjures up a poetic paradise. Stretches of golden sand against a blue sky and a blue sea are standard images in tourist brochures. These places do exist. I've seen and even sat uncomfortably on some of them. But the vast majority of the world's million kilometres of coastline is not even remotely like that golden image. Coastlines are typically rocky, muddy, strewn with pebbles, garbage and filth, oil pollution and plastic washed up from the sea. The shore is more often a place of danger and death than a playground.

Some authors have portrayed the beach like this, as a symbol of endings and lost causes. *On the Beach* is the title of a 1957 nuclear war thriller by Neville Shute, in which the beach becomes a metaphor of desolation and loss. The expression "On the beach" means washed up, hopeless, finished. Beachcombers and beach bums are losers, people you wouldn't want to invite to your wine tasting event even if they wore masks. In J.G.Ballard's apocalyptic novel, *The Terminal Beach*, the beach represents the end of everything.

In H.G.Wells's *The Time Machine* the world ends on a lifeless, darkening beach.

What attracts so many to the beach, I'm sure, is a very different kind of symbolism, unconsciously felt. It's not about the sand, it's about the sea, the sight and sound and clarity of the ocean. The sea is our primeaval home, and we long to return to it. When our local beaches were reopened a woman interviewed by the local radio station caught it precisely in three words: "This is freedom." The sea can lead to anything and everything. If I sailed out from Long Island I could get to Tahiti eventually, and become another Gaughin; or maybe to the Greek Islands, and become another Henry Miller, or *anywhere*, to become *anything*. From the edge of the sea we can touch the whole world, or leave it. All our troubles are literally behind us. That is freedom.

First broadcast: July 6, 2020

Prophets of Doom

One of the many annoying things about the COVID-19 affair is that it has brought out of the woodwork an apparently unlimited number of people who pretend to know the future. "What will happen next?" they ask breathlessly, and go on to offer their empty wisdom with all the confidence of Old Testament prophets. Some anticipate the apocalypse and have stimulated a lively market in old nuclear bunkers and survival gear. Others predict a kind of post-industrial economic collapse and a return to nature with a vestigial population of survivors. None of them has the slightest idea what will really happen because it hasn't happened yet. Now, as always, it's open season on the future. Anyone can imagine anything, and they do.

We don't like uncertainty about the future, we much prefer magical thinking. Prophets have always found an audience because it's only human nature.to want to know what's going to happen next. Since the dawn of time we have been plagued by false prophets with Tarot cards, star charts, palm reading, crystal balls, dice and sacrificial entrails. In the long dark ages before Twitter almost anyone with a white beard and an impressive manner could set up as a prophet. The sixteenth century French astrologer Nostradamus became and still is famous, although the vast majority of his prophecies were incomprehensible or wrong.

Now even the white beard is not required. *Anyone* can set up as a prophet. So we find ourselves listening to financial advisers, think tanks, opinion polls, fundamentalist preachers, TV astrologers, market researchers, the Federal Reserve, new age gurus, the CIA, newspaper columnists, and two billion social media users with nothing better to do than spend their time imagining futures that will never happen. They are happy to speculate on the basis of almost no facts and an unlimited number of unknowns, a practice technically known as guesswork.

When my younger self complained about things that went wrong, or that didn't turn out the way I wanted, I was told that life is full of surprises. This turned out to be absolutely true. Few things that we expect actually happen, and a great many things that we don't expect do happen. Life is nothing but surprises. Enormously important events like COVID or Trump usually catch us unprepared. For example, Bastille Day in France commemorates the anniversary of a minor riot in Paris that became a revolution and turned the world upside down. Did anybody see it coming? No. Did anybody foresee the War in Vietnam or the collapse of Communism? No, and no. Life is full of surprises. A few voices in the wilderness had predicted some kind of virus epidemic, but they were ignored. This is the fate of all true prophecies, because they are invariably inconvenient, and usually disagreeable. Early in 2020 the US government was vigorously trying to suppress statistics on the spread of the epidemic.

Prophets are well aware of this. They know that the future is infinitely flexible and adapt their message to their present audience. From the earliest times kings, princes and other insecure rulers have employed soothsayers who, like fairground fortune-tellers, would tell them only the good news about their future victories, their future wealth and eternal glory. Soothsayers bearing bad tidings had better look for another job. In this respect things don't change much at the top levels of government.

But to engage the attention of ordinary, skeptical citizens like you and me a prophet must focus on the bad news. Nobody believes good news. We know from experience to expect the worst. So our popular mass media prophets must be a pessimists with catastrophic tendencies, full of dark and negative predictions. These creeps have no more real knowledge about the nonexistent future than anybody else, but they have discovered the key to making money out of people's natural anxiety.

The only ones who feel *uncertain* about the future seem to be those scientists who prefer to work with facts rather than emotional fantasies. Science can offer predictions of two kinds: forecasts based on scientific laws, for example, that water will boil at 100° C at sea level, or more speculative forecasts based on long-term trends like obesity or global warming. In the absence of scientific laws or long-term trends any statements about the future are mere fantasies.

All prophecy harks back to ancient religious traditions in which the future is already predestined, foretold in the sacred text or written in the stars: Kismet. This makes any kind of prophecy a complete waste of time. We can sit back and enjoy fate's roller coaster. But if you don't believe in fate or prophecy, and if you *really* want something to worry about, listen to the scientists.

First broadcast: July 13, 2020

A Quiet War

There is a generational war at least once in every generation, because the old guard and its old ideas must be replaced. That's how we move ahead, and that's one difference between human beings and animals. In the animal kingdom there are few changes over the years or centuries. This generation of young chimpanzees or young whales is very much like the last generation, and the next. They follow the immemorial habits of their species. Humans are different. Older people like me imagine they know how the world should be run and how civilized people should behave. But we are, of course, completely wrong and out of date, and must be pushed aside to make way for the next generation who have quite different (though equally mistaken) ideas about how the world should be run and how civilized people should behave. This process of exchanging one set of illusions for another is known, not without irony, as "progress."

My own generation didn't stand a chance in our particular generational war. We were just beginning to get our young lives in focus after 1945 when the Baby Boomers came thundering in to obliterate us—an enormous cohort of eager kids who immediately started inventing things we had never heard of like long hair and sex and rock and roll and political protest. We pre-boomers were overwhelmed and quickly written out of history.

The COVID-19 epidemic has given a new spin to the generational wheel of fortune. Young people are confronted with an almost unprecedented upheaval in their lives, and all the restrictions and changes are coming from above, from those same old people who are so despised, out of date, out of touch and, let's face it, boring. The effect has been to put a brake on young lives just when they should be accelerating to maximum speed. Education, sociability, sports, love, and sex have all been put on hold. It's hard to imagine anything more frustrating, and the cracks are beginning to show. Already we've seen riotous gatherings and threatening fireworks in the night, unruly unmasked assemblies of young people in bars, on city streets, and on beaches.

On my daily walks I've noticed that, in contrast to the middle aged and elderly, virtually no young people are wearing masks. It's a quiet rebellion by one generation against another. The thought is quite literally in the air that there's no point in protecting senior citizens, and young people might be better off without them. Youngsters aren't afraid of death, because they scarcely believe in it for themselves. The eighteenth century essayist William Hazlitt wrote a famous piece on "The Feeling of Immortality in Youth," which is as true now as it was then. "No young man believes he shall ever die" he wrote, which may be an exaggeration but certainly captures an essential truth. Risky activities just don't seem risky when you are young and feel invulnerable, and it's obvious that masks and social distancing seem oppressive and ridiculous to most teenagers.

Generational conflict is as old as history. Long before COVID-19 came along there was a justified resentment about the gigantic national debt that was and is being loaded on to the shoulders of future generations. Now the debt will be much, much bigger. Thomas Jefferson believed that there should be a redistribution of wealth in every generation, on the principle that "The Earth belongs to the living." Now we are doing the opposite—impoverishing the young for the benefit of the old. The young certainly have something to be resentful about. Some may even have been made more rebellious by closure of schools and colleges, and the heady taste of freedom that came with it.

A plague that targets the old and spares the young has been a standard trope of futuristic science fiction. After their liberation the young survivors have a wonderful time going back to barbarism—but barbarism with plenty of modern machines, unlimited fuel, weapons, and electronic gadgets, mysteriously provided by someone else.

A few years ago Christopher Buckley published a novel called *Boomsday* that predicted the next inter-generational war. In the story an angry young blogger suggests that the unproductive and expensive Baby Boomers be given incentives to make a graceful exit at the age of seventy. The proposal takes off on the Internet, and inspires angry demonstrations at golf courses, retirement communities, pharmacies, and other places sacred to the elderly. If you want to find out how the story ends you can get the book from the library, or you can just wait.

First broadcast: July 20, 2020

Life on Wheels

There are so many vague and disturbing predictions about what life will look like after COVID-19 that I thought it was time to weigh in with something clear and definite. I predict that, in the future, we will live even more in our cars.

This is not guesswork but a forecast based firmly on a long, steady trend. Cars have been moving into the center if our lives for over a hundred years, ever since Henry Ford's Model T showed that everybody could have one. There are almost two cars per person in the US. Cars have taken over the cities, created the suburbs, and defined how most of us live. Kids get to school in them, adults drive to work, and everyone drives to the shops or on vacation. The car is like the famous credit card: we don't leave home without it. City dwellers pretend to despise the automobile, but they are getting out of the cities as fast as they can, and there are no subways in Wyoming.

We have adapted to pollution and enormous traffic jams, to the discipline of highway driving, and even to 36,000 accidental deaths a year when the discipline fails. We love our cars. They offer us refuge and a quiet space, gifts that are increasingly hard to find. Many commuters, in the old days, used to look forward to this as the one peaceful time in their day. But you don't need to commute, or even to drive. You must have noticed, as I have, cars that stay parked for long periods, occupied by one person. In the privacy of a car nobody can hear your unauthorized phone conversations, or comment on your taste in music. The family can't see you ruining your diet or taking a long nap. An air conditioned car parked in an attractive spot is the ultimate freedom capsule. It fulfills the second promise of the Declaration of Independence, "Liberty," and possibly even the third "The Pursuit of Happiness." Two out of three is not bad.

In the age of COVID-19, a car is also the ultimate Personal Protection Equipment for you and your family. If you stay in your car you're safe—apart from the other drivers. The world is adapting. We have curbside pickup, drive-in movies and concerts, drive-in churches, and drive-in virus testing. When this thing is over we may never abandon our wheels again.

Cars, like their drivers, have become larger and larger so that we now have an epidemic of automobile obesity. The tank-like SUV is now the most popular style, loaded with equipment for entertainment and comfort, and more and more like a mobile home. A bathroom is the only missing accessory, and no doubt that will come soon. We are already halfway to living in our cars. Some ingenious people have found ways to work from their cars using cell phones and internet connections, so that "working from home" may soon take on a whole new meaning.

One of the most striking pictures to come out of the epidemic was a color photo from *The New York Times*, shot from above by a drone. It showed people lining up at a food bank in Texas. We've all seen those heartbreaking pictures from the Great Depression of ragged people lining up in the rain on the sidewalk for food handouts in the 1930s. This

Texas food line was different. It consisted of hundreds of cars that, on close inspection, appeared to be new or nearly new vehicles. Here's a paradox: people lining up for free food in cars that must each have cost tens of thousands of dollars. I understand that these people were suffering real hardship (life is full of surprises), but you could say that it is progress compared to 1930, when almost everyone waiting for food handouts was a pedestrian. Now even poor people are rich. It shows how thoroughly the motor industry and the banking industry between them have captured our hearts, our pocketbooks, and even our common sense. An economist might ask how long this economic model can be sustained. But, while we wait for an answer, the shining SUV can at least take us in comfort to the breadline.

First broadcast: July 2, 2020

The Triumph of Parkinson

There can rarely have been a confirmation of any social law as complete and comprehensive as this. After months of lockdowns, stay at home orders and confused warnings about indoor and outdoor activities, I think we can claim that Parkinson's Law is finally vindicated and can stand alongside the law of gravity and the first law of thermodynamics as an established scientific fact.

I have a faded first-edition copy of *Parkinson's Law*, by C. Northcote Parkinson, which I bought in 1957 when I was a mere teenager, and which instructed me in some of the most important facts of social and sociological life just when I needed them most. The statement of Parkinson's Law, and the evidence for it, appear boldly on the first page.

"*Work expands so as to fill the time available for its completion.*" *General recognition of this fact is shown in the proverbial phrase: 'It's the busiest man who has time to spare.' Thus, an elderly lady of leisure can spend the entire day in writing and dispatching a postcard to her niece in Bognor Regis. An hour will be spent in hunting for her spectacles, another in choosing the postcard, half an hour in a search for the address, an hour and a quarter in composition, and twenty minutes in deciding whether or not to take an umbrella when going to the post office in the next street. The total effort that would occupy a busy person for three minutes all told may in this fashion leave another person prostrate after a day of doubt, anxiety, and toil."*

Parkinson's Law explains many things: why retired people always seem to be in a hurry in spite of having nothing to do, and why government agencies take twice as much time and five times as many employees to accomplish almost nothing. In a bureaucratic organization (and this means almost any modern organization with more than a handful of workers) there is no relationship at all between the amount of work to be done and the number of staff required to do it. Unlimited time means unlimited delay. Each thing to be done increases in importance and complexity according to the time available.

For months now some of us have had extra time on our hands. We've not been shopping, commuting, or socializing. Our days have become much longer, and Parkinson's Law has begun to manifest itself at home. Anecdotal evidence shows that most of us have not relaxed and taken a long vacation but have created more complicated and more time-consuming work substitutes to fill our empty time. It's not what you do that matters, as Parkinson would say, it is how long you take to do it.

Spring cleaning is a good example. By the end of May millions of houses and apartments must have been so clean and tidy as to be virtually uninhabitable. Closets have been turned out and many long-forgotten horrors revealed. Even a few garages have received the makeover treatment. Backyards and front yards have been trimmed and replanted to the edge of perfection like the royal gardens at Balmoral.

Consider a nameless senior citizen whose pre-Covid domestic assignments included filling and cleaning the bird feeders—a task occupying a few minutes every couple of days. Suddenly, with extra time on his hands, he discovers that the job is much more complicated than he thought. The varieties of seeds for different birds have not been thoroughly researched, the feeders are not well chosen or well placed, the squirrels have become intolerably bold. Catalogs must be studied, new equipment ordered, and in no time at all the innocent task of feeding the birds has become virtually a full time job, and vastly more expensive.

Ancient hobbies have re-emerged, like bird watching and watercolor painting. In the basement I found a kit for carving decoy ducks, consisting of a lump of wood, a knife, and some little pots of paint. I haven't stared on this project yet, and I hope I don't have to. One magazine advertised scale model working steam engines that you could build in your living room if your wife would let you. Other advertisements have promoted cheese making, calligraphy, exotic embroidery and cookery projects, and beer making kits to help us recover from all the rest. Parkinson's Law always comes to our aid. Even the smallest activity can and does expand into a time-absorbing work project.

It seems that we can find plenty to do when we have nothing to do, but the enthusiasm doesn't necessarily last. At the beginning grocery stores nationally reported a sharp increase in the sales of baking equipment and gourmet cooking ingredients. But we were soon back to white bread and canned beef stew. In April there was a 37% rise in the sale of lace underwear. It has not yet been reported how long that particular passion lasted, but we can speculate.

When we think we see a glimmer of light at the end of the COVID-19 tunnel the question will be: can we get back up to speed again? We will go forward into the post-epidemic era sparkling clean, tidy, well organized, with plenty of lace underwear. But what next? After having so creatively wasted our new leisure time, will we want to get back to wasting our time on mere work?

First broadcast: August 3, 2020

Professors in the Cloud

As colleges and universities prepare for the new semester a huge question mark hangs over the whole process of higher education, and indeed education in general. Can distance learning be made to work? New technologies mean that students no longer need to meet in boring old classrooms with professors who may or may not be the best and the brightest. They also won't need to waste their nights and ruin their livers at keg parties, or resist the moral temptations of the mixed dormitory. They will be like scholar monks of the middle ages, alone in their cells with their holy laptops.

Even if it works, and perhaps especially if it works, distance learning offers a dim prospect for the academic community as a whole. Redundant professors will have to learn how to hang out at the beach, and all the young people who planned to go to college and have a thoroughly good time by abolishing social distance will be bitterly disappointed.

In the interests of full disclosure, I confess that I taught some college-level undergraduate courses on the Internet back in the 1990s when the technique was still in its infancy. So, just for once, I do know what I am talking about. The experience made me skeptical. From the student's point of view, it may be a quick and easy way to stack up credits. But it is a horribly impoverished substitute for an educational experience to sit alone with a computer, insecurely connected via the internet to a professor you don't know and linked to your unseen fellow students only by artificial, laborious online discussions or Zoom sessions. I doubt that anyone will remember a great Zoom session, but the best live lectures and tutorials stick in your mind forever.

Plenty of professors dislike online teaching, but are equally reluctant to go back to the campus and the classroom where masks and distancing may be rejected by some students. As for the students themselves, their motivation is hard to guarantee when everyone in the virtual classroom is only a click away from his or her e-mail, or a video game, or something even more interesting. It demands a lot maturity and self-control, which may be no bad thing if it happens. But it may not happen. Honest testing and evaluation are almost impossible on the Internet and, from the teacher's point of view, the main problem is that you don't *know* your students. You can't look at them directly, or talk to them, directly, or make all those delicate connections that can only be made face to face. In fact, you have no idea who is behind the screen on the other end, or where they are getting their information. I have come to believe, along with many old-fashioned educators, that more distance equals less learning.

At kindergarten it may be possible to teach via videos, like Sesame Street. But you can't hope to accomplish higher education for teenagers by having them watch a more intellectually elevated version of Sesame Street. Somewhere along the line independent thinking has to enter the picture, and this is where I dare to introduce an old fashioned, almost forgotten teaching tool, cheaper and infinitely more flexible than a computer—the book. When you come to think about it, a book is the perfect example of what we want from distance learning. It's completely portable, virus-free and doesn't even require power or a high-speed internet connection.

Just about all the knowledge in the world is available in books, and we have done very well with them for five hundred years. There are literally millions of excellent books still out there, written by experts on their subjects, that will bring students closer to the ideas and mind of the writer that they could ever get to their professor in a big lecture hall, or even to Professor Big Bird on the small screen. A computer course, like a movie, is only the inferior shadow of a much better book. Books deliver the distilled essence of a subject,

Some skills inevitably demand a lot of hands-on instruction. Pure book learning is unlikely to produce doctors or aeronautical engineers we can trust. But the vast majority of what are usually called "academic" subjects, where actual competence is of no importance, can be self-taught from books with no more than a little written or recorded guidance, like an old-fashioned correspondence course. If facts and information are what you want, the pursuit of knowledge is wide open and free. If a certificate is what you want, you are doomed to tangle with the higher education industry, whatever form it takes.

Before tens of thousands of college students are swept away by the dream or nightmare of higher education on the Internet, let's pause for a moment, reflect on the costs and the options, and consider going back to the books. Where do you think professors get all that stuff?

First broadcast: August 10, 2020

The Rugged Individualist

America has always been famous for its individualism, the idea that every person should be free to live in his or her own way. This romantic myth originated with European philosophers in the 18th century, and quickly made its way across the Atlantic where it was eagerly embraced. This was a new nation ready for new things and, with a vast territory and a small population, it seemed like the ideal testing ground for this revolutionary idea of individual freedom.

So history unrolled through the nineteenth century as a gigantic carnival of individualism: the robber barons, predatory capitalism, the survival of the fittest, massive political corruption and, out west, the cowboys and all they symbolized. To Europeans it looked like anarchy, the absence of civilization rather than a new civilization. But in due time things settled down and most Americans became and still are well-integrated members of their community, like any German, or Frenchman, or Chinese, or African.

But the romantic myth of individualism has lingered on, with sometimes disastrous results. It has been endlessly recycled in movies with the figure of the lone hero (or more rarely heroine) following a tradition that goes back to ancient Greece. But in real life (whatever that is) all of us, heroes included, are part of society whether we like it or not. We are formed by society from the moment we're born: pressured to conform at school, where nothing is worse than being a "loner," and bombarded all our lives with media messages promoting the same standardized images, roles and ideas. If we decide to break out of the strait jacket of conformity we are immediately embraced by another group of conformists. For example young people today who claim to be different and better because they are "woke" are simply conforming to the kind of rigid political correctness that some of us remember all too well from the 1960s when the activists were described by one observer as "Studiously conformist in their nonconformity and obedient in their rebelliousness."

Freedom is a different matter. We have many private areas of free choice: what to wear, drive, say, what caliber of gun to carry, and so on, which are important but don't change the fact that we are social creatures. In fact we are more social and sociable than we ever were.

Individualism has been blamed for the failure to control the Corona virus, because the American response to the epidemic has been uniquely chaotic and ineffective. But there just aren't enough individualists around to have such an impact. They are rarer than the proverbial hen's teeth. The fashionable anti-government, anti-science movement is in fact is no more than another kind of conformity, what George Orwell called Groupthink. The epidemic has made it rather obvious that what a great many people really want to do is to submerge themselves in the comfort of the crowd: a packed beach, a motor cycle rally, a rave party, a night club, or even a mob, because they want to do what everyone else is doing and think what everyone else is thinking. This is normal behavior.

Sociability is one of the strongest human instincts. It is just unfortunate that, at the moment, it is dangerous.

    A true individualist, if any exist, would have an advantage here. He or she would enjoy solitude, which is richly available and desirable. Never have there been such good reasons to seek solitude, and so few reasons to join a crowd. In a famous poem John Donne wrote: "No man is an island…" a cliché that is profoundly true. But sometimes an island, even if it is only a fantasy island, is the safest place to be.

First broadcast: August 17, 2020

The Loneliness of the Long-Distance Consumer

When the first big department stores opened in cities around the country they created a whole new way of shopping. Buyers could browse a huge range of goods in a warm sociable indoor ambience that was entirely safe, and almost domestic. You could see and touch and even try on the goods, and discuss them with sales staff—it was a fully interactive consumer experience and even a kind of entertainment. Department stores were an immediate success, as were the suburban malls that appeared in the mid-twentieth century to provide much the same shopping experience outside the big cities.

Everybody of a certain age has memories of department stores. I remember as a child what a treat it was to be taken to astonishing places like Harrods in London. On my first visit to New York I was greatly impressed by Macy's. As this rich shopping culture disappears, as it seems to be doing, we have suffered an significant loss. It's not so much the "consuming"—we can do that on the couch—but the fact that traditional shopping provided somewhere to go, and people to see. It was a sociable and even an aesthetic experience.

These days most of our stuff arrives in cardboard boxes, and sociable shopping is not the only thing we have lost. The choice is necessarily much smaller. We make our list—for food for example—and the store sends us what they have in stock, with some substitutions. This adds an element of mystery to our daily diet, and can lead to some culinary adventures, but it's not the same as seeing, touching and choosing the food for ourselves.

In the declining days of the Old Soviet Union there was a joke that people would join any line outside a store without knowing what was being sold. They knew it must be *something*, and something was better than nothing. The huge GUM department store in Moscow, which I visited in the 1970s, was a strange sight in those days, with a great many staff and room after room of empty shelves. The Soviets did not believe in spoiling their citizens with too much choice.

Retail companies are now in the same position as the old Soviet government. They have an unprecedented amount of power over what we eat, drink, wear, read, and see. We are in effect like astronauts on the space station. We are at the mercy of ground control, and we get what they send us. So I wondered whether this new supply-side economy might have a bright side, some gentle social engineering that could improve everyone's life.

Food is a good example. Supermarkets are the department stores of food, and offer the same cornucopia of choice. We all know we should improve our diet, but sometimes the temptation is too much. If nutritionists were inserted into the food supply pipeline we would get kale instead of baked beans, salad instead of steak, and nutritious grains instead of pizza. Booksellers would deliver only educational and politically correct books instead of celebrity memoirs. When it comes to buying clothes online the retailers could do a lot to improve our choices. Many people are seduced by slender models in catalogs, but they often do not possess a mirror, especially not a three-way mirror. A three-way mirror saves many time-consuming trips to the post office with returns. We could send our exact dimensions and other biometric data with pictures to the retailer, and they would choose garments that are fitting and flattering. I can imagine Alexa and her creepy electronic friends becoming more authoritarian about everything—no more airline tickets to unapproved destinations, no trivial popular music, and absolutely no serious information about anything.

We may have lost the department store with its cozy atmosphere and infinite variety of free choice, but we may be on the edge of gaining an invisible big sister who will guide our future shopping choices and make sure that everything, absolutely everything we buy, is good for us.

First broadcast: August 24, 2020

Pumping Irony

Gyms and fitness centers suffered worse than almost any other business in the big COVID-19 shutdown, being among the first to close and the last to open. They were thought to be the most dangerous places for transmission, but in New York they opened again at the end of August.

This must have been be a great relief to those who, unlike me, take their fitness seriously. During the early part of the shutdown there was a big demand for home gym equipment including a mysterious thing called Kettlebells. "Clients are afraid that all their work will go to waste" said one gym owner. The quest for fitness is often described as "work" rather than fun or pleasure, and indeed it seems strangely self-punishing because there is no end to it.

I remember being fit once, almost exactly sixty two years ago. It only lasted a few weeks and happened after we had finished basic army training, during which we were made to run or march around carrying heavy weights, climb over impossible obstacles, and do unreasonable numbers of push-ups. At the end of this hellish experience I was stronger and fitter than I had ever been before or have been since. I wish I had taken a picture. Immediately afterwards I reverted to my normal state of unfitness and stayed there.

From time to time I have felt guilty about this, and a few years ago I summoned up the courage to join a local gym. This was a mistake. They tried to sell me a lifetime membership, but that would have been a bad deal at my age so I took a free trial membership. It was a friendly place. A lot of the clients showed no signs of actually exercising. They treated the gym as a social club, gathering around a table in the lounge to chat and eat donuts.

Beyond the lounge, the gym itself was a more intimidating place—a big room crammed with heavy weights and elaborate machines with names like "abdominal crunch" and "chest compressor" reminiscent of medieval torture instruments. Fortunately a member of the staff steered me away from these and put me on a treadmill where I walked, just the way I walk every day outside. After about half a donut's worth of walking I left. That was the end of my trial membership at the gym, and I have never looked back.

The last time I achieved fitness in 1958 it was thanks to a particularly nasty sergeant from the army physical training corps. We had no equipment apart from him, and no subscription was necessary. The modern machinery of fitness seems excessive, although the flashing lights and electronic monitors must make it more entertaining. But I'm sure that mowing a large lawn with a hand mower, or raking leaves, or shovelling snow, is as good an exercise as you can get in any gym. After all, how healthy and fit do we need to be? If years of exercise enable you to build up powerful muscles and impressive stamina, what are you going to do with them? People who do hard physical work are already fit, but most of us are sedentary or even supine workers, especially if we are working from home. No muscles are required.

What must keep people coming back to the gym, apart from the companionship and the donuts, is the heady sense of superiority you get as you walk out the door into the world of feeble, non-exercising mortals. For a moment, you feel strong, and powerful, like Superman, or Superwoman. As illusions go this must be one of the best, and well worth the cost of the subscription.

First broadcast: August 31, 2020

College on Hold

Labor Day is a paradoxical holiday, dedicated on the one hand to the history of work and labor unions, and on the other hand to fun and idleness. But on the first Labor Day in 1852, work and fun were part of a single celebration. First came the parade and serious speeches from union leaders, and then a big picnic and concert to round the day off. This year just about everything has changed. The Trade Union movement represented worker solidarity, which just what we don't have at the moment with millions out of work, or working at home, or in the so-called gig economy. They are, quite literally, on their own. As for the picnic and the concert, social distancing has put an end to them. So today is just a date on the calendar, when the post office will be closed and people will take advantage of the three-day weekend to stay at home and not visit their relatives.

Some of the biggest losers are college-age students. For tens of thousands of teenagers this would have been the first of many weeks away from home and family, as they settled into college dorms and began the process of metamorphosis from awkward high school students into sophisticated graduates. Entering your first dorm room must be a truly magic moment. At last you have your own space, away from parental supervision and you are free to make your own mistakes, including mistakes that your parents were not even smart enough to think of. At college you will meet thousands of other newly-liberated teenagers. This will be the party of a lifetime, which is why parents have good reason to be paranoid at this time of year.

Colleges and universities are in a state of complete uncertainty about how to handle COVID-19, but most of them have opted for online teaching. In other words, no dorm room, no big party, and no escape from the family. It must be a huge disappointment. Staying at home in your room in front of a laptop is no substitute for the college experience. We could be in danger of creating a generation of solitary, unsociable teenagers like the self-isolated *Hikkimori* of Japan or the *Honjok* ("alone tribe") of South Korea.

The good news is that college, unlike school, is not compulsory. College can wait, for years if necessary, as it did for me and for the eight million veterans who benefited from the GI Bill to get a late education after 1945. College at seventeen or eighteen is not fate, and it may not even be the right thing at the right time. There are plenty of other choices, some of them much more interesting as I can confirm from personal experience. A lot of successful people have jumped off the educational conveyor belt for a while without ruining their lives.

A surge of late-entering students a few years from now would cause disruption in the higher education system, of course, but there's already plenty of that. Unemployed professors could occupy themselves meanwhile by writing the definitive academic study of their subject that they have been putting off for the last several decades, so everyone would benefit.

Colleges and universities need to guarantee that students who take a pandemic sabbatical for a while don't lose out on the place of their choice. They should receive vouchers like those we get (if we're lucky) for postponed airline flights, allowing them to return at any time within (say) ten years. In ten years they will be too old for the twenty-four hour party, too mature to waste their time playing football, and just the right age for serious, and safe, higher education. If there is any good to be squeezed out of the COVID-19 disaster, this may be it.

First broadcast: September 7, 2020

What Would Victory Look Like?

It's now more than six months since most of us started re-arranging our lives for the convenience of the coronavirus—cancelling meetings, vacations, work, school, and much of our personal lives. It feels as if summer ended before it began, and here we are sliding towards winter.

The questions on everyone's mind are: how do we get out of this mess, and how will we know when we are out of it? What would victory over the virus look like?

When a problem is out of control the traditional political answer is to declare victory and leave the field. This has been the American strategy in Iraq, Afghanistan, Syria, Vietnam, and everywhere else where foreign adventures have gone badly. It's a good strategy if the problem is far away, because the chances are that nobody cares. It is not so easy when the problem is right here at home, and in our homes, and everybody cares.

An epidemic is not a war, but the same old political strategy will probably be used, and is being used: suppress the statistics, insult the journalists and the experts, confuse everyone with fake facts, and finally declare, in the face of all the evidence, "We've won."

Victories are important psychologically, and we celebrate them for a long time whether they happened or not. We celebrate victories in war, in business, in sports, in politics, and even victories over ourselves, for example in overcoming an addiction. An ideal victory has a clear and definite result. There are winners and losers, although over time we may forget which was which. Many Americans believe that the Vietnam War was a victory. Those who were in Saigon in 1975 will tell you that this was not the case.

So what would victory over the virus look like? The virus has no plans, and no intentions, and fights no battles. But, as in a war, there are only three choices: complete victory, complete defeat, or containment. It is very hard to eliminate a virus once it is well established, so the best we can hope for is containment, in which the enemy doesn't go away but stays around, ready to fight another day.

A premature declaration of victory could therefore be worse than defeat. Consider the Greek King Phyrrus of Macedonia, who was known for being aggressive, proud, and reckless. He really enjoyed a good fight, as long as he survived it himself, and didn't worry about the casualties. In the year 280 BC, he won a great battle against the Romans, but at such a high price that both armies were virtually destroyed. King Phyrrus got to boast about it, which was what he really wanted. But the victory cost too much, and the Romans had their revenge later.

That's where we get the phrase a Phyrric Victory—a victory that turns into defeat. A declaration of victory over the virus, when all we have is containment, would be exactly like that. The politicians will claim a triumph, but the virus cares nothing for political rhetoric and will carry on as if nothing had happened. Having celebrated our false victory in the usual sociable human way, we could end up echoing the rueful words of King Phyrrus as he contemplated the destruction of his army: "One more victory like that," he said, "and we are finished."

First broadcast: September 14, 2020

No Respect

The third Monday in September is Respect for the Aged Day in Japan, but not here. On this special day the Japanese return home to visit and pay respect to their elders, and volunteers in their neighborhoods participate by making and distributing free lunch boxes to older citizens. Entertainments are provided by teenagers and children, and special nostalgic television programs are broadcast.

We don't have a Respect for the Aged Day for the obvious reason that, as Rodney Dangerfield liked to say, we don't *get* no respect. There is a Grandparents Day in September, but if you are just plain old and not a grandparent you are out of luck. Nobody sends flowers or a card, still less a free lunch, although anyone who has survived all the hazards of life for so long surely deserves some recognition. I've been told, by very senior seniors, that things used to be different, and that age used to command respect. Their memories must be playing tricks. Old people get less respect nowadays than old cars or old furniture, which at least may have monetary value. When did you last see an old person, however well-preserved, valued at tens of thousands of dollars in the Antiques Road Show? We admire ancient trees, elderly cats and historic buildings. What about historic people who are a living link with the past, and can even remember what life was like before the Internet?

The old have archaic skills that may come in useful when the Internet collapses under the weight of Zoom meetings. We can teach the young folks how to write, and even how to read, without a computer, how to change a typewriter ribbon, how to send a message of any length using nothing more expensive than a piece of paper and an envelope, how to entertain themselves without video games or social media, how to take pictures without a smartphone and even how to make phone calls without one. Some talented people of my generation could and did run whole radio stations without a computer anywhere in sight, flew planes around the world without computers, and found their way from place to place using paper maps. But will anybody ask us to share these ancient skills? They will not.

What the aged get is not so much respect as resentment: because our vulnerability to COVID-19 creates problems for everybody else, because we are a burden on the Social Security and Medicare systems, and because we have cornered most of the money and real estate. No wonder we are unpopular, and irritating as well. We fail to remember our ever-changing passwords, fall victim to childishly obvious online crimes, read books, punctuate correctly, and drive too slowly. It must be maddening for the younger generations. I know the ignorance of the old used to drive me crazy when I was young. But, as Mark Twain put it: "When I was a boy of fourteen, my father was so ignorant I could hardly stand to have the old man around. But when I got to be twenty-one, I was astonished at how much he had learned in seven years."

This is a youthful society. Many adults seem to have abandoned the idea of growing up altogether. But, paradoxically, it is getting older all the time. Almost fifty million citizens are over sixty-five now, but there will be ninety-five million by 2060 or about a quarter of the whole population. So a few hard-working young people will (with luck) be supporting a *lot* of old people. If we get any respect at all in this situation it will have to be self-respect. And the great thing about self-respect is that we can have as much of it as we like, without ever having to explain why.

First broadcast: September 21, 2020

The Last Frontier

Christopher Columbus was fortunate to live in what we now call The Age of Discovery, when there was still plenty to be discovered. Five hundred years later what we see on the world map is what we get, now and forever. Modern explorers are left with nothing to explore except a few muddy ocean depths and the remotest corners of the remotest forests and ice fields. The unfortunate fact that the world is round and finite, and not flat and infinite, means that, everything has already been discovered, mapped, and overpopulated.

Even when Columbus sailed the ocean blue in fourteen hundred and ninety two he didn't expect to find any *unknown* lands. His map showed the great ocean to the west of Europe with a few islands scattered in the middle of it, and China the East Indies on the other side. These were believed to be places of fabulous wealth, a profitable earthly paradise where Columbus expected to land. Instead he bumped into San Salvador.

History rarely lives up to our myths. We celebrate Columbus as the Great Navigator, the discoverer of the New World. But he never set foot on mainland America. He even missed New Jersey, which is hard to miss. And nobody told him that the American continent had already been discovered thousands of years before by nomadic Asiatic tribes crossing over the land Bridge from what is now Russia. It was discovered again five hundred years before Columbus by a bunch of blond Vikings in funny hats who decided it was not a very rewarding place and went home.

Columbus, like most migrants, hoped for fame and fortune, but was disappointed. Returning from his first voyage he vastly exaggerated the wealth and desirability of the places he had found—an early example of fake news—in order to raise money for his next voyages. He was appointed Governor General of the newly discovered Caribbean territories. But he behaved with such brutality there that he was recalled to Spain in disgrace, where he eventually died in poverty and obscurity. If I hadn't failed Latin at school I would be tempted to remark *sic transit Gloria mundi,* but I won't.

Christopher Columbus has a lot to answer for. He and his patron Queen Isabella, set a pattern of bad behavior for the whole western world. In different ages this behavior has been called piracy, economic imperialism, prospecting, entrepreneurship, gambling, and corporate capitalism. But the basic motivation has always been the same passion that urged Columbus to undertake his dangerous exploits. According to one of his biographers, Columbus was driven by a 'Burning desire to acquire riches, power and fame.'

Half a millennium later Columbus is remembered as a hero rather than an avaricious predator, and the results of his restless voyages have been momentous. Consider what the world would have been like if Lief Ericcson and Columbus and the rest had just stayed at home, if *everybody* had just stayed at home to cultivate their gardens. History would be utterly changed. That blank space in the western ocean would have remained blank, and Native Americans, not decimated by smallpox and white invasion, might still be living an Arcadian life across this beautiful continent, hunting and eating buffalo burgers. All the hyphenated-Americans would be living in their old countries with their old cultures, and speaking their own languages. The American Revolution of 1776 would never have happened, and so the French Revolution of 1789 would very likely never have happened either. France could now be ruled by King Louis the twenty-fifth, which might be an improvement.

What Columbus did achieve, entirely by accident, was to open up a vast new western land frontier for European exploitation—seventeen million square miles of prime real estate, completely empty except for the people who happened to be living there. This enormous territory was explored, mapped, tamed, bought, sold, suburbanized, and politicized over the next five hundred years. In the glory days of the frontier millions of immigrants spread westwards over the Alleghenies and into the Great Plains, looking for land, freedom, and a pot of gold at the end of the rainbow. Some made it all the way to California, thinking that the far west must be an earthly paradise, just as Columbus believed it was. They arrived at the Pacific, and that was the end of the frontier and the dreams that went with it. It's no accident that Hollywood is the place of dreams. It is located exactly at the point where dreams must give way to creative script writing and special effects.

A frontier, even an imaginary one, is a safety valve and a challenge. In the past there was always a new frontier open, until suddenly there wasn't. The inescapable question was, and is, what next, where next? The least promising answer seems to be outer space. Billions are being poured into Mars exploration vehicles. Three were launched in 2020, and Elton Musk has a plan to put a colony on Mars by 2050. He can count me out. Mars, even at the equator, is colder than an English seaside resort, and has virtually no modern amenities. And if we ever did get to Mars we would take our troubles with us, just as Columbus and the westward migrants did. Mars would inherit our diseases, our flawed governments, our irrational prejudices, and our pointless wars. Mars doesn't need that.

If we can't find a new planet, or a new frontier to cross on this one, we have a few things to work on right here and now: toxic politics, inequality, the environment, and much more. With all that frustrated frontier energy, we could make this old Earth great again.

First broadcast: October 12, 2020

A Safe Place

Now that the election is over we can return to more traditional and less stressful forms of entertainment, like murder. When the evenings draw in and the temperature falls with the leaves, there's nothing as comforting as a good murder. The actual homicide rate in America has been going down for a long time, but in movies and on television it has gone the other way. Movies were always violent, ever since the earliest cowboy epics. Now they are more violent by far. By the age of eighteen, according to Mr. Google, the average citizen has watched forty thousand murders on the small screen.

Fortunately some TV producers have discovered a way to make murder more fun, if not for the victim then at least for those who enjoy it at second hand. Most of these good-humored murder stories come from Britain, Australia or Canada, perhaps because the chance of actually being murdered in those countries is very low indeed, so that the event can be watched without anxiety. American murder stories tend to be much darker, and the Scandinavians are relentlessly grim, perhaps because of their freezing weather and long, dark winters when murderous thoughts multiply in the shadows.

The most enjoyable murders are typically set in the temperate zone, in reassuringly stylish and civilized past, and in delightfully picturesque places. If you believe these tales, every charming English village is a war zone with a murder (or several) once a week. I'm talking about popular and endlessly repeated Public Television series like Midsomer Murders, Father Brown, Poirot, Miss Marple, and a dozen others.

What makes them funny, and not grim and gruesome like real violence, is the invariable formula that, as it were, sanitizes the killing, and provides an ending in which the culprit is revealed and justice is served. The formula calls for a detective, professional or amateur, with a comical or incompetent sidekick, a disagreeable police chief, and a medical examiner who, unlike most real medical examiners, is often female and beautiful. There is a love interest, and a plot that almost always involves a vast inheritance, romantic jealousy or some betrayal in the distant past. Nobody seems to have a regular job, so they can devote all their time entirely to constructing ludicrously complicated crimes that would baffle Mr. Holmes himself.

Even more comforting than these lighthearted TV mysteries are the classic detective novels on which they are often based. In the golden age of the murder mystery, the twentieth century, mostly female authors like Margery Allingham, Agatha Christie, Dorothy Sayers, Patricia Highsmith and P.D.James crafted a formula that never fails. The crime happens in a closed world that is almost cozy, and certainly more understandable than the chaotic world outside. The cast of characters is limited and familiar. The fatal blow is regularly found to be struck by a left-handed assassin, the blackmail note is almost always typed on a machine with a distinctive damaged letter "e", and the detective is always struggling with a hidden weakness or a secret sorrow. The absence of cell phones and computers means that the detective has to work much harder to fathom the mystery, and so does the reader. There is always a surprise at the end, but not a big enough surprise to give you a heart attack.

But where are they now, those satisfying murder mysteries with their quirky characters, intricate plots and not-very-surprising endings? The *New York Times* bestseller list is full of dismal tales about terminal illness, divorce and victimhood, horror stories, and corporate thrillers about making money. There is scarcely a good murder story anywhere in sight.

The decline of the murder mystery must be a symptom of the decline of murder in general—not the *quantity* of murders, which is more than adequate, but the *quality*. The murders we read about in the newspapers every day never have the rich complexity of the classic detective story. How often do we hear of a notorious criminal being murdered on a train, which is stuck in a snowdrift, by a conspiracy of all his past victims, each of whom strikes one blow with the knife, and the mystery is solved by a famous Belgian detective who just happens to be on the train at the time? (The plot of Agatha Christie's *Murder on the Orient Express*).

This sort of thing almost never happens these days, even on the Long Island Rail Road. Murderers just take out a gun and shoot somebody they don't like. They devise no plot, leave no false clues, and display no subtlety at all. It is boring for newspaper readers, even more boring for detectives who might fancy themselves as equals of Hercule Poirot or Sherlock Holmes. Modern murderers have no class, and murder itself has become routine and dull, so who wants to read about it?

Fortunately we can reach back into history and borrow many of the classic murder mysteries from our local library, or buy them at bargain prices from one of many online sellers of secondhand books. The volumes are usually old and rather battered, which adds to the pleasure of reading them because it is evidence that you are part of an invisible book club. Many other people have enjoyed trying to guess the ending to the same story.

The worst that can happen while reading a good detective story is that you can't put it down, and waste a whole afternoon discovering something that you should have guessed in the first ten pages. But real life rarely provides so much dramatic action with so little risk, or with such satisfying dénouements. A good old-fashioned murder mystery makes life worth living.

First broadcast: November 16, 2020

Sitting Out the Pandemic

As winter creeps up on us many of our habits change. We stay indoors more, eat more, and exercise less. This is exactly the kind of thing that the propagandists of the fitness industry keep warning us against. Most senior citizens have been hearing this same old refrain for half a century or more. We have heard it all and ignored it all before, and we're still here.

There's no doubt that the COVID-19 fiasco has slowed life down, quite literally. At the beginning the streets and parks were full of newly-enthusiastic joggers and walkers, and stores specializing in fitness equipment were sold out so that you couldn't buy a set of weights or a stationary bicycle anywhere. The fitness craze didn't last long. Now the streets and parks are mostly empty, and there is an enormous amount of secondhand fitness equipment for sale on E-Bay. We are embracing the new normal, which means moving much less. There are no meetings to go to, no stand-up social events, fewer big stores to walk around or car parks to walk across. What we are doing instead is a lot of sitting.

This is clearly an opportunity for some of us to shine. I have always had a talent for sitting and, over the years, it has matured into a kind of genius. I can and do sit on anything: flat rocks, leather armchairs, park benches, office chairs, recliners and just about any object that will support the grateful human anatomy. It's hereditary. My mother and grandmother were both champion sitters and both lived to be a hundred.

Since the energetic life of the hunter gatherers gave way to the more static life of farming, humans have invented many devices to improve the sitting experience: the rocking chair, the bar stool, the overstuffed armchair and, for a final sit, the electric chair. This could be called a fundamental activity of our species, and not to be despised or neglected.

Historically, sitting has been the superior position. A king or queen sat on a throne, while the courtiers stood around. Aristocratic soldiers sat on horseback, while the ordinary troops marched. Even now, in some traditional schools, pupils stand when a teacher comes into the classroom, and in some corners of society we still stand for ladies when they enter, and politely find them a place to sit. If you want to feel good about yourself, sitting is the way to go.

The only trouble with sitting in the modern world is that it gets no respect. Somehow, perversely, sitting has become associated with idleness. Yet most of the work of the world is done by people sitting down, like our three million government civil servants, and untold numbers of computer programmers and office workers. At home, every new technological gadget encourages us to sit more and move less, from the old fashioned remote control to fully automated wireless home in which just about everything can be controlled from your armchair. Voice-operated systems save even the effort of pressing a switch or a button. Everything is geared to minimal movement, zero physical effort, and so we sit.

Sitting needs to be recognized as an activity like any other, and perhaps even as a sport with Olympic potential, because sitting performance can be measured. Fitness enthusiasts monitor their daily exercise by carrying a little electronic gadget somewhere on their bodies that tells them how far they have moved, how fast, how many calories they have used, and so on. The results, I'm sure, give them a feeling of achievement and superiority. There's nothing wrong with that, but it leaves the rest of us with nothing to brag about.

There must be an entrepreneur willing to finance a new gadget that would allow us to measure and be proud of our new lethargic lifestyle. It could be called the SITBIT. With two triple A batteries inserted, and attached to the appropriate park of the anatomy it would measure your total sitting time, so you could boast about it later via Skype to your other sedentary friends. The SITBIT would allow you to count your hours of sitting at the end of every day, and see how many calories you saved by not moving. If you added the hours spent sleeping and subtracted the total from twenty-four, any time left over would count as exercise, even if it was only creeping from the armchair to the bed. With a bit of luck that number would be very close to zero. In our new post-exercise world, you too could be a winner, without ever leaving your comfy chair.

First broadcast: November 30, 2020

The Unanswered Question

There is a piece of modern music by Charles Ives called "The Unanswered Question." That's an intriguing title because we all have a whole lot of unanswered questions. Unfortunately the music only *asks* the question, with its strange dissonances and unsteady rhythms, without offering even the hint of an answer.

So we are left with all our unanswered questions unanswered, including the biggest one of all at this time of year: what do you want for Christmas? What do *they* want? What does *anybody* want?

Children have no problem with this question. They have lists of wants, readymade by the advertising industry, downloaded directly from the web and delivered to Santa Claus on the Internet. But the older we get the harder it is to know what *we* want, that's my experience. It's easy enough to look through the closet and decide that you could use some socks, or to choose a book or a CD. But what we really want—that's a huge, terrifying, existential question, and most of us don't like to think about it.

E. B. White, a fine writer, has a short story called "The Second Tree from the Corner," in which he seems to answer the question like this: we *do* know what we want and it is so inexpressible, so unfathomable, that we can never quite see it clearly, let alone say it in words or get it gift-wrapped from Amazon. This seems to me very perceptive, and explains why we have to invent things to want that turn out to be unsatisfying because we don't really want them at all.

There are certain universal wants, I suppose, like the proverbial health, wealth, and happiness. Many men, including me, would like to be taller, braver and stronger. Many women would like to be shorter, thinner and blonder. We would all like to be smarter. None of these things can be ordered from Amazon. They would be great gifts, if we could get them, but still they are only shadows of something else that we don't have a name for.

If we don't know what we want ourselves, how can we possibly guess what other people want, even those nearest and dearest to us? Gift cards are a kind of solution, but they simply toss the smoking bomb into the hands of the recipient, who then has to worry about what *they* want. Some people ignore the whole impossible question of who wants what and just pass unwanted gifts along more or less at random from one year to the next. It's efficient and practical, but scarcely generous.

Most of us don't want or need any more stuff, and one way to avoid wasting money on unwanted gifts is to give something invisible, intangible, but that just about everybody *does* want which is, in some small way, to do good in the world. One year my wife gave me a fine flock of ducklings destined for a village in Africa. I never met these ducklings personally, but I often think about them, and hope they made somebody happy. Charitable gifts like this have several advantages: they don't need to be wrapped, they never have to be returned to the store, and they are always exactly the right thing because they help somebody, somewhere. After all, in the true spirit of the season (if we remind ourselves what that is) it's not what you get, it's what you give that counts.

First broadcast: December 13, 2020

Happy Winter Solstice

One of the few things I like about the month of December is that, at this darkest time of the year, The Holidays give us something to celebrate. When we light the Christmas tree or the Hanukkah candles, we are recapitulating thousands of years of human history. The winter solstice tells us that we are over the worst of the darkness, if not the worst of the winter. Ancient peoples made great efforts to get the date of the solstice exactly right, because they were naturally fearful that the sun might never come back. Stonehenge is just one example. It's the biggest and heaviest calendar in the world and it really only tells you two dates: the summer solstice in June and the winter solstice in December.

Ever since these special moments in the year were identified they have been celebrated. The Babylonians had *Sacaea,* their winter festival of renewal. The Romans of classical times had their *Saturnalia,* a sort of extended Happy Hour. It was an unabashed orgy of eating, drinking and spending, and perhaps in its excesses came the closest to what we now call The Holidays, which isn't surprising given that Roman culture was in so many ways similar to our own. We imitate their architecture and their ruthless politics, so why shouldn't we copy their winter celebration? The Scandinavian and German peoples have their Yule

Feast, a more staid version of the same thing. These winter festivities are among the oldest of all human traditions. It would be a shame to give them up now.

I like way decorated houses light up suburban darkness, although I have reservations about inflatable Santa Clauses and plastic reindeer with flashing noses. I used to enjoy the sense of community that The Holidays created back in the pre-Covid era. It was a time to be sociable, and even convivial. We'll have to wait a while before we try that again. Let's hope we haven't forgotten how to do it. But we still can privately enjoy the food and drink of the season. All kinds of special treats come out of the closet: rich cakes and puddings, extravagant cookies, and drinks that we'd scarcely dare to try at any other time of year. Every rule of health and nutrition is abandoned, and that feels so good. In my mostly abstemious family decades ago, Christmas was permission for our numerous aunts and uncles to imbibe lethal drinks like port, egg nog, Tia Maria, Crème de Menthe, and even brandy, with results that were very gratifying for a young boy to see.

I especially love the sense that, just for one day, the frenzy of life will be switched off. Some stores can't resist opening, but December 25th is mostly very quiet outdoors, magically quiet, whatever family dramas may be unfolding indoors. In Europe this period of calm is much longer. People make a week of it between Christmas and New Year.

What drives me crazy about this season is exactly what drives most people crazy—the frenzied commercialism of it all. By the middle December, we're ready to scream "Scrooge was right!" I hate the bowdlerization of beautiful Christmas music by the recording companies. The same old carols are played on every conceivable instrument, from the banjo to the saxophone to steel drums and the penny whistle. Every imaginable type of choir is wheeled out to bring a bit of novelty to the old favorites. We are assaulted by amateur choirs from small towns, children's choirs, exotic choirs consisting entirely of Patagonian Transvestites or Buddhist monks, ethnic choirs, Democratic, Republican and Mormon choirs. If this doesn't give the old carols enough spin they are played or sung very fast, as if the whole ensemble is on speed, or more often with excruciating slowness, and tortured into every pop style from jazz and rock to rap and hip hop. Who needs or wants any of this?

There exists, for example, a glorious rendition of "Silent Night" by the choir of King's College Chapel in Cambridge. That's enough. We don't need fifty more. We don't need "Silent Night" played on cowbells or electronic synthesizers, or sung by the Spice persons or the Dixie Chicks or Snoop Doggy Dog. Enough is enough. Christmas should be a happy time for everybody, not just for the deaf.

At Christmas we are encouraged, and indeed almost required to be merry and joyful, which doesn't come naturally to most of us. My dictionary defines merriment as "Mirthful, full of animation, and slightly drunk." I don't mind being cheerful. We all have a social duty to be cheerful. But merriment is an expectation too far. It is even harder to be joyful. Joy is rarely seen these days, except in TV advertisements, where whole families are routinely overcome with joy at the sight of a new car or some other commercial object of desire. These TV actors are hired perform joy so the rest of us don't have to. For non-professionals, displaying joy or merriment in a public place, especially on the first day of winter, is likely get you arrested, and quite right too.

The ancient Druids may or may not have been merry and joyful but, five thousand years ago, they took immense pains to calculate this turning point of the year because it meant that time was, as it were, on time, and that the seasons would continue. Winter must come and, in the immortal words of Percy Bysshe Shelley, never a man to avoid a cliché: "If winter comes, can spring be far behind?"

First broadcast: December 21, 2020

Organizing the Future

It won't be a Happy New Year unless we have provided ourselves with one essential life-enhancing item: an appointment book. They're sometimes called agenda books, or diaries, or organizers. But organization is the last thing I need, I don't have an agenda, and I gave up keeping a diary years ago when I realized that everything was repetition. I favor a particular brand of appointment book with rather beautiful covers, because I expect to see it every day for three hundred and sixty-five days. It is designed in Britain, distributed in Canada, and of course made in China. The size, five by seven inches, is just right. It's not so small as to reduce my life to insignificance and not so huge as to suggest an excess of self-importance, and one year at a time seems a reasonable period to anticipate, encompassing four seasons, one birthday, and fifty two garbage collections on Tuesdays. A year may be a little optimistic at my age, and given the way the rest of the world is going. But they don't sell six month or three month versions.

Simply buying an appointment book made out of paper marks me as hopelessly out of date, a living memorial to Johannes Gutenberg. Most people these days prefer to entrust their futures to tiny plastic gadgets, also made in China, which will keep all their plans and notes safe unless and until the thing stops working, or the batteries run out and their futures vanish. I was shown one such device that allowed the user to actually write on the screen, just as if it was a piece of paper. Paper was invented by the Chinese two thousand years ago. The wonders of progress never cease to amaze me.

The advantage of a plain paper appointment book, apart from its simplicity and cheapness, is that it is a visible, tangible token of optimism about the coming year. Appointment books unlike diaries, record the future not the past. They tell the story of your life before it happens. If you have a whole year of dates waiting to be filled in then you might as well get busy and fill them in, so that your year is laid out in a reassuring manner, like a rather dull novel with no surprises. You can even indulge in a bit of pre-emptive nostalgia by writing in things like vacation dates and other eagerly anticipated events like retirements and hip replacements. It's not exactly a guarantee, but a conditional promise that good things will happen or, at the very least, that *something* will happen. The future becomes more real when we write it down with dates and times attached. Indeed, there are moments when the future seems more real than the present, and infinitely more real than the past.

An appointment book must be somewhat provisional. We can't pretend to know exactly what will happen in the wider world in 2021, any more than we knew what was coming in January 2020. I had to make several changes in my planned schedule that year, and perhaps you did too. For all we know, in 2021 a trade war with China may cut off our supply of little electronic gadgets, and the batteries to run them, and even paper appointment books. Confusion will be complete. Nobody will know what they are supposed to do or where they are supposed to be from one day to the next. But I already have my appointment book fully organized right through December 2021. What could possibly go wrong?

First broadcast: December 28, 2020

Taking the Short View

A New Year should have something special about it—a sense of expectation, and a fresh start. But this year seems different. Nobody is building any new utopias. Quite a few are building bunkers.

Just about every greeting card we received this year expressed the hope that 2021 would be better. The twentieth century was such a horror show, with two world wars and numerous other catastrophes, that we had high expectations of the twenty-first. But the first twenty years of this century have been a bit of a disappointment. It wasn't supposed to look like this.

The Founding Fathers thought a lot about the future. "What will posterity think of us?" they wondered. But the word "posterity" has almost vanished from the language, and even the idea is no longer fashionable. It's too remote, too far in the future, and we don't want to think about it, so we don't.

That, in a nutshell, is the secret of optimism—short-term thinking. Politicians are brilliant at this. They never look beyond the next election or fundraiser, so they are always hopeful and never feel the need to actually *do* anything apart from fundraising and electioneering. Posterity can take care of itself.

The rest of us have to *learn* short-term thinking for the sake of our own mental health. Any competent psychologist will tell you that the world is divided into optimists and pessimists, worriers and non-worriers, and our place on the scale depends on how and how much we think about the future. At one extreme a truly dedicated pessimist, like those hiding in bunkers in North Dakota, will gaze into the far future and anticipate all kinds of horrors, not for posterity but for themselves: new viruses, political chaos, global warming, civil war, the return of Donald Trump to The Apprentice, and the collapse of civilization generally. This cannot fail to create gloom and despondency. At the other end of the scale a natural optimist, like *Mad Magazine's* Alfred E. Neumann, will just glance at the clock and wonder hopefully what's for lunch. It's all a matter of time scale.

In other words, to guarantee a Happy New Year, we can and must live as much as possible in the immediate present, as many Eastern religions recommend. And not just Eastern religions: that genial eighteenth century letter writer the Rev. Sidney Smith advised that the secret of happiness was to: "Take a short view of life, no further than dinner or tea." This is a piece of conventional wisdom we can all understand. Live in the moment. Pessimists may cry that the party's over. But it's not over *today*. This is the fourth day of 2021. So far, so good.

First broadcast: January 4, 2021

Help Is on the Way

We don't get to see much of the mighty universe here in the suburbs. But out in the deep countryside, or out to sea, away from the glow of street lights or any lights at all, the stars shine very bright. We get the view that people had for thousands of years, before streetlights and illuminated Christmas decorations blotted out the night sky—billions of stars spread out across the sky from horizon to horizon. It still takes your breath away. Looking up at nature's fantastic planetarium it is tempting to imagine other worlds and other lives out there. The earliest civilizations found prophetic messages in the stars. Now we look for something different: a kind of salvation, or at least some useful advice.

The collapse in 2020 of the giant Arecibo radio telescope in Puerto Rico, that scanned the galaxy for alien radio signals, was a blow to many scientists and amateurs interested in the search for extraterrestrial intelligence. Funding for this kind of research is hard to find. Politicians are naturally alarmed by the possibility of any kind of intelligent alien life arriving here, because aliens can eventually become citizens and vote. But the search continues on a smaller scale, and the *idea* of intelligent aliens remains immensely appealing: over fifty per cent of Americans claim to believe in them. Consider the recent flurry of news stories about a strange glow out in the remotest part of the universe where no light should be, as if some unimaginable entity had left the bathroom door open, and about odd radio signals from our nearest star, and the discovery of a mysterious monolith in the desert. It's all pure Hollywood, which of course is where our images of aliens come from. They tend to be small and cute like ET, or nasty-looking and dangerous like Darth Vader. We hope that the small cute ones will arrive on earth first.

The main argument for the existence of intelligent life in the universe is the sheer *size* of space. My way of thinking about it is to imagine leaving the earth on the space shuttle, escape velocity twenty thousand miles per hour, and going on at that speed for a year, beyond the solar system, then another year, another ten, another hundred, another thousand, another million, another trillion years. After all that you would still be in the universe, with no end in sight. How would you expect it to end—with a white picket fence? And over the fence, what?

How likely is it that so much valuable real estate remains uninhabited, and that we on our speck of dust are the only living things in it? Infinite means infinite, and on an unlimited number of stars with planets it must be true that there are an infinite variety of creatures. Some of them must have learned the secret of travel between the stars, so we can imagined (and have imagined) that the universe is teeming with life forms, some of them considerably smarter than the not very bright Luke Skywalker, and able to travel between the stars. There are half a trillion stars in our galaxy, and nobody knows how many other galaxies. It's hard to believe that all the infinite worlds in infinite space have produced nothing more intelligent than us. If so, the universe would have been a complete waste of time.

When and if the space aliens finally find us they may bring advanced technologies that will allow us to turn back climate change, or find new sources of clean energy, or get decent reception on our cell phones. They may bring advanced wisdom that will release is from some of our crazy, self-destructive beliefs and obsessions, and solve some of our most pressing problems like campaign finance reform and term limits on Congress, although that might be too much to hope for. If Hollywood is any guide our space visitors will certainly bring advanced forms of violence. An external threat always helps to unify a group, a nation, or a planet, and that might really be our salvation.

But the aliens have not contacted us yet. Or perhaps they have found us and checked us out. Then, like a fisherman with a disappointing catch, tossed us back into the great sea of annoying and silly life forms that undoubtedly inhabit the universe, and continued on to look for something more interesting.

A 2020 Hollywood space opera starring George Clooney didn't feature any aliens at all, helpful or otherwise. It was about finding a new home and a fresh start for humanity on one of the moons of Jupiter. Clearly, this was the right fantasy at the right time. Our galactic visitors, if and when they arrive, may be looking for a new home for themselves, having ruined their own planet. In the worst case scenario, they could be aliens in such desperate trouble that they will be asking *us* to save *them*.

First broadcast: January 18, 2021

Goodbye to All That

It has been said, rather too often, that in the past year we have been living through history. But we live through history all the time, as long as we live at all—we have no choice. Even the supposedly boring 1950s were history. We had the very real threat of nuclear war, and Senator Joe McCarthy's attack on democracy, and the even more imminent horrors of Rock and Roll to worry about.

History is what has been written down. No written record means no history, or what we call prehistory when plenty was happening but we don't know what. People who lived in prehistory missed their chance of being a part of the record, but they never knew, and never cared. Even most history is forgotten almost as soon as it happens. Presidents, pop stars, and pandemics come and go, leaving only a few lines in old books and a few fading memories. In the long term we retain only the edited highlights. We know, or think we know, that a thousand years ago, in 1021, King Henry of France invaded Italy, although not why, and that five hundred years ago in 1521 Henry VIII executed the Duke of Buckingham for treason. That must have made the headlines. The human story, seen through the historical record, is one, long, murderous soap opera. Ordinary lives and ordinary people like you and me, or at least like me, are scarcely mentioned. We are mere spectators of the perpetually repeated drama in which really important people fight for wealth and power.

Even so, I think, we would like the events of our own lifetimes to be dignified as History with a capital H. The unlucky year 2020 was documented in the most intense detail in every imaginable medium—not just dry written reports for scholars but videos, interviews, and live news reports on every disaster, every calamity. There is no shortage of information for future historians, and no shortage of lessons for future generations.

But when it comes to learning lessons of history the entire human race gets an F. It may be that we simply don't want to know too much about our past, or at least the darker parts of it. As the teaching of history fades away in schools and universities, each new generation will remember less, and care less, and understand less about what they quickly learn to dismiss as the "old days." They will get their history from the movies. Only the most dramatic, colorful, or romantic moments make it into the movies. The past becomes more digestible when it is simplified, scripted, tidied up, populated with big-name stars, decorated with a love interest, dramatic settings, and perhaps (as in the case of Alexander Hamilton) music and dance. Who knew anything about the Trojan War before Brad Pitt joined in, or that Mel Gibson put so much energy into the cause of Scottish Independence in 1298? Film makers can do what they like with history. The people who lived back then don't care, for reasons that it would be impolite to mention.

The ancient Greeks believed that history was cyclical: there are no new plots, just the same stories repeated over and over, like the programming on some public television stations. The truth is that human nature never seems to change. There was never a plague without plague deniers, never a new scientific discovery without science deniers, and never a failed leader without his faithful followers. As an example of history's endless repetition we certainly ran true to form in 2020, and into early 2021, when the Capitol was invaded by a white fascist mob. There was much talk of "unprecedented events," although the Capitol had been stormed at least twice before in 1814 and 1861. The end of the election, predictably, was chaos. But that is usually the outcome of any human conflict in any period of history.

The past year was so confusing, so full of contradictions and conflicting plot lines, that I really don't understand any of it yet.

I'm waiting for the movie to come.

First broadcast: January 25, 2021

PART TWO

A TOXIC ELECTION SEASON

American Politics after 2016

> *"Donald Trump is a phenomenon that foreign countries haven't seen. So it is a shocking experience to them that he came in to office."*
>
> **Henry Kissinger**

> *"In fact the US faces problems that the Founders would sadly have recognized: irrational political extremism; the push of religion into government even as public involvement in politics has declined; foreign entanglements that tempt Americans to sacrifice their own values; and persistent conflicts over race and gender and class and immigration, all too reminiscent of dark episodes from the past."*
>
> **James Macgregor Burns**

If I understood what happened in Washington DC in 2016 and 2020 I would be happy to tell you. But it would be easier to unravel the inner workings of the Politburo or the Central Committee of the Chinese Communist Party. Chaos is an effective form of cover for whatever is really going on. Here's what we can guess from the outward signs.

In 2016 Donald Trump was elected by a minority of the popular vote further manipulated by the irrational rules of the Electoral College. A weak and unpopular opponent combined with a huge expenditure of money plus covert support and interference by the Russian government produced this unexpected result. But, after a moment of hesitation, Trump ran with it and surrounded himself with a gang of sleazy, often criminal officials from the ultra-right (a dozen had already been indicted, arrested or imprisoned by the summer of 2020).

Trump had and has an almost cult-like following, with support from about thirty percent of American voters. To be seen on TV in America is already to be next to a god. To be a celebrity on TV is to become an actual god. To be rich into the bargain is to be rise above the gods. All this plus his loud and intimidating manner, and not least the name "Trump" seem to have convinced many voters that he was the man to shake up the system and speak for the 'little guy.' This was a more dramatic demonstration of false consciousness than even Karl Marx could have imagined.

Trump was responding to a real and dangerous phenomenon: a large, disappointed and fearful section of the population that felt (correctly) that it was being left behind by economic progress and marginalized by the liberal focus on minorities of all kinds. The novelist William H. Gass speculated that Trump tapped into the "slightly hidden fascism" of the American working class. He certainly activated their not-at-all-hidden racism. Enemies had to be discovered, and Trump has uncovered them wholesale.

The 2016 election also showed the institutional weakness of democracy in America, as many commentators observed. It was never a model democracy of any kind, but extreme corruption and foreign interference revealed how open it was to an authoritarian takeover by a man who was willing to break all the rules.

At the same time the election sparked a global problem, as a score of pseudo-populist authoritarian leaders were elected by following his example. This twenty-first century form of populism promises a kind of 'retrotopia' that looks back to an imaginary past when men were men, and minorities and women were kept in their place. Its leaders have, of course, little intention of pursuing any such policies.

Progressives and liberals brought this on themselves by their relentless focus on identity politics, collective guilt, and the rights of any and all minorities. The big issues, such as massive inequality, monopoly, climate change, international conflict, have been more or less ignored by both sides. But Trump grabbed the big issues that guaranteed *his* support: fear, resentment, and patriotism. Equal rights for LGBDQ persons, though no doubt admirable, is not an effective political answer to "Make America Great Again."

We have ended up with a toxic mix of extreme identity politics on the left and the possessive individualism of market fundamentalists on the right. What the philosopher David Hume called "partisan zeal" obliterated both self-interest and common sense, and reflex tribalism became the pattern of American politics.

The Reagan era of American conservatism promoted a simple-minded attitude that could be summed up as: "Don't worry, be happy." Trump promoted a completely opposite and more dangerous attitude in his followers: "Be proud, be angry," but without offering them any reason to be proud, or any way of turning their anger into political action apart from supporting Trump himself.

The November 2020 election, with an exceptionally high voter turnout, gave a solid victory to the Democratic candidate Joe Biden. Trump immediately denounced it as a fraud and joked about "Not giving up the White House." But he doesn't make jokes, and he may have meant it, in which case he was seriously contemplating a Third World style *coup d'état*. Either way, Trump the angry man may not be the main issue, but rather the more or less criminal people who have come to power on his coattails and the apocalyptic political atmosphere he has created. Pandora's ballot box inevitably comes to mind.

The endgame included a mob invasion of Congress on January 6, 2021, incited by the President, and a Congressional call for his impeachment (again) or removal by way of the twenty-fifth Amendment. On January 20, in an anxious Inauguration under heavy security, President Joe Biden and Vice-President Kamala Harris were sworn in, and Donald Trump flew off to Florida. It is anybody's guess what will happen next.

A Little History

Monsieur de Tocqueville Spots the Problem

"I do not know if the people of the United States would vote for superior men if they ran for office, but there can be no doubt that such men do not run."
Alexis de Tocqueville

The United States temporarily escaped the ideological fanaticisms of Europe, but at a price that was clearly seen and understood by Alexis de Tocqueville in the 1830s. From the earliest days of the republic, America's civil religion demanded conformity to three propositions contained in the Declaration of Independence: that all men are created equal, that they have inalienable rights, and that the sole purpose of government is to secure those rights. These propositions—all of them palpably incorrect and at least two of them obviously silly—come together in a kind of philosophical Bermuda triangle, within which any attempt at clear thinking swiftly sinks and vanishes.

The dilemma of American politics is neatly encapsulated here. The doctrines of equality and individual rights represent the highest moral and political aspirations. They signal civilization at its highest pitch of idealism. Yet not only are they impossible for any human government to put into practice but, if they were even attempted, they would lead directly to the revolutionary destruction of the social ties that make civilization possible.

In this context, the eternal debate about rights and duties is of the very highest importance, although it easily lends itself to the most Neanderthal kind of conservative agenda. The framers of the Declaration of Independence, the Constitution, and the Bill of Rights lived in a different political universe. They *assumed* the existence of some reciprocal ties of duty and obligation between individuals and communities. The strong doctrine of individual rights was designed to redress the oppressive balance of the old European power system, in which a citizen had almost unlimited duties and no rights worth mentioning. De Tocqueville concluded that there was an inherent struggle in America between two opposing impulses: the spirit of rugged individualism versus the contrasting spirit of community and association-building.

Starting from the fine intentions of the founders, the spirit of possessive individualism gained the upper hand and finally obliterated the notion of duty altogether. If self-interest is the only universally agreed good, and if the laws of the market are believed to maximize the self-interest of every individual, government is left with no role at all. The American political system is unique in the extent of its powers and in its inability to use them. Two of the most fundamental conditions for civilization are that a state must control its own borders and must also monopolize the means of violence. The government of the United States cannot even begin to manage either task. The borders are so porous that a million "illegals" walk through every year, and the means of violence so widespread that mass murders with assault weapons are becoming a commonplace news item. Drugs, of course, are virtually an uncontrolled free market.

This is no territory for the amateur philosopher. The finest thinkers for three centuries have failed to square this circle: freedom *versus* order, positive *versus* negative freedom. It comes down to an ideological conviction or simple faith. Old-fashioned Marxists and new-fashioned dictators both assume that "the people" suffer from false consciousness and must be forced to conform to certain rules to guarantee social stability. Liberals and libertarians assume the opposite—that society must be structured around what people say they want, and that social stability will arise naturally from the satisfaction of needs. There is not much historical evidence for either position. The balance of rights and duties seems to originate from communities, not governments. A functioning community is the utopian ideal that, in theory at least, would allow individual freedom without also creating chaos.

The United States never developed a native language of community or public duty that would allow politicians or citizens to say: "this is intolerable," *and act on that belief.* These individualistic and (frankly) anti-social assumptions have been molded into popular culture, so that most young Americans today grow up with an image of community as a stifling set of restrictions, and public duty as a convenient cover for graft. For them, government is no more than an Ombudsman — a source of rights, freedoms and protections for each separate individual against all the rest.

National life teaches its own poisonous lessons about interdependence and belonging. Pervasive corruption at every level of politics and law makes nonsense of the sense of public duty or citizenship. Since 2016 the notion of politeness or dialogue in politics has been all but abolished, and we have seen an explosion of intolerance about race, as well as a resurgence of justified but dangerous feelings of hate and envy caused by economic inequalities (what the existentialists termed *ressentiment*.) It seems impossible to reach a consensus about the most basic social problems because nobody is willing to pay the price of collective responsibility. Urgent issues like crime control, housing, national health, welfare, education and old age are subject to the "every man for himself" rule. American society is a mirage promoted by political phrase-makers; it does not exist in the minds of Americans. Where the "social" is meaningless so is the future of society, or at least its continuation in the same form.

The form we call Democratic Capitalism has been a stunningly successful experiment, creating economic security and a better quality of life for at least half the world's population, along with a large measure of personal freedom. No other political/economic system has come close. But the qualifier "democratic" is essential. In the first century or so of capitalist development the system was so authoritarian and fiercely exploitative that Karl Marx came to believe that it would destroy itself.

Capitalism *without* democracy will work and does work. It has the potential to turn the clock back to the days of the robber barons. Russia and China are good examples. When politicians become nothing but the *apparatchiks* of capitalism, democratic control will soon evaporate. We saw it fully displayed in 2020 when the barefaced criminality of large companies like Wells Fargo,

Volkswagen and Purdue Pharma took us right back to the most exploitative phase of capitalism. The grotesque concentration of wealth that results from the monopoly of huge markets is bound to increase pessimism and resentment, offering an opening to false populists like Donald Trump. The unravelling of American democracy can be dated unambiguously to 2016, when the robber barons took power and everyone else was left behind.

Plato at the Polling Booth

"Democracy, a charming form of government, full of variety and disorder, and dispensing a sort of equality to equals and unequals alike."
Plato, *The Republic*

Democracy is a glorious idea. The notion of free citizens governing themselves by electing the best and the brightest people among them as representatives is one of the best notions that the human race has ever produced. It's a pity that the results are so often disappointing—especially that the chosen representatives so seldom appear to *be* the best and the brightest.

Public cynicism is at an all-time high. About half of all citizens just don't bother to vote. Democracy, as Winston Churchill remarked, is the best of bad choices among systems of government. The problems are huge, and not just the obvious problems of campaign contributions, and the need to make a forced choice between two ideologically blinded parties.

The problem with democracy is that we do it to ourselves, so can hardly blame anyone else. Plato always elbows into this argument. He identified the big problem two and a half thousand years ago when he labeled democracy as "Rule by the appetites." He wasn't talking about fast food, although he might have been. Plato argued that democracy gives us so many options that the system inevitably drifts towards mediocrity, instability, paralysis, decadence, and finally to chaos and tyranny.

Plato's argument, in a nutshell is that the first principle of democracy is freedom so that, in a democracy, anything that limits personal freedom is resented. Nobody likes restrictions, and nobody loves authority. For that reason, nobody wants to exercise authority either. Politicians, anxious to keep their comfortable jobs and self-inflated salaries, are strongly motivated to pander to popular whims. When freedom rules, teachers become scared of their pupils, and parents become like children themselves to avoid the responsibility for disciplining their offspring. Democracy creates the feeling that nobody's in charge, or that everybody's in charge. Either way, each one of us is on his or her own, at the center of the universe. Nobody else matters much. There are so many conflicting demands that the system cannot deal with them. Nobody can clearly tell right from wrong or even admit that there are such things. All standards and regulations are progressively abolished in the name of freedom. Random violence occurs but, because freedom is so important, nothing much can be done about it. Citizens become disillusioned with politics and stop participating. Eventually, democracy falls apart.

Some modern theorists argue that Plato was completely wrong, and that we have far too *little* freedom in our democracy, being oppressed by millions of laws and regulations, taxes, and government bureaucracies. This is encouraging. When two groups of experts disagree so profoundly, we must assume that the truth lies somewhere in the middle.

But, if we are living in Plato's last stage of democracy, which he called the age of appetites, there is some good news. Plato gave it as his opinion that this is the most enjoyable time to be alive, simply because we have so much personal freedom. The main thing is to save our fragile system from moving on to the next stage of the cycle: the age of tyranny.

Of course, Plato was an ancient Greek with authoritarian instincts who lived in the very first age of democracy, which didn't last long. In terms of his own chaotic era and the Athenian political system, he was proved to be absolutely right. His case against democracy was that we citizens are just not capable of governing ourselves. We are too greedy and selfish, and not very smart, and we choose representatives just like us, but even greedier. So (said Plato) a few superior people must take on the difficult task of governing the rest. Plato's Republic was based on totalitarian rule by wise philosopher kings who governed for the common good.

The idea of philosopher kings makes us smile, especially now. Imagine a society run by the philosophy department at your local university and you might want to laugh out loud. But if we forget the antique language and think about the central idea: those who govern should be the most thoughtful, intelligent and most honest people who can be found, it doesn't sound too crazy.

I reflected on this while we were having breakfast in a suitably elevated location, at the top of the Sheraton Hotel in Boston. This offers a panoramic view of the city, overlooking the Charles River towards the noble buildings of Harvard University and the Massachusetts Institute of Technology. What a concentration of brainpower there must be in these two square miles. If only all that trained intelligence could be harnessed to solving the problems of the world we would surely be on our way to utopia. The only problem I can see is that people with these qualities would not become politicians at any price.

It is a pure Platonic fantasy, of course. But consider that every responsible profession except politics demands rigorous training, an examination of competence, and a code of ethics. Politicians need no qualifications: they get into power simply by making themselves popular, and that was Plato's whole complaint about government by and for the people.

Tweak the system just a little, and the problem might vanish. We could require a few appropriate qualifications for political office. These are some of the best jobs in the world, with by far the best lifetime benefits. Surely, at the very minimum, those who govern a society of almost three hundred million people, with global power, should have excellent educational backgrounds? Not professors, heaven forbid, but men and women with enough intelligence (including emotional intelligence) and practical training to understand the economic and social sciences, to know at least something about the physical sciences, and (perhaps most important) to understand history. They should also be acquainted with at least a couple of foreign languages. It's a complicated world out there.

This would reduce the field of candidates by about ninety-nine per-cent, and it should be further refined by a few basic psychological tests. Many large companies use testing to weed out unstable and unsuitable applicants for the most responsible jobs, and the tests are much more sophisticated than they used to be. They can measure aptitudes like teamwork, honesty, psychological stability, and commitment to the ultimate goals of the institution. When it comes to the US government the goals would presumably include those high ideals written into the Declaration of Independence and the Constitution.

After their educational backgrounds had been checked, and their psychological testing completed, the highly qualified candidates could go forward to the election, with their educational achievements and psychological test scores posted on the polling machines for all to see.

One final thing: I'm sorry about this, but the money will have to go. The Supreme Court decision of 2010 essentially sold the US government to the corporations and the oligarchs. The old joke about "The Best Congress that Money Can Buy" became a plain reality. If politics was really about the polity (citizens) instead of money, then a very different group of people would want to participate in it, and they might be the people we need.

Frankly I think this is a brilliant idea, worthy of Plato himself. All we need to do is to persuade the next democratically elected Congress to pass it into law.

A Modest Proposal

Of all the many things we have to worry about, foreign interference in the next election cycle seems the easiest to solve if we start early. Anyone of retirement age knows how to solve it, but many younger people simply won't listen because the solution seems so weird to them, and perhaps even wicked.

When we go to a polling station we vote on a computer. It may be via an optical scanner or a touch screen, but somewhere along the line our vote goes into a computer and is then transferred to other computers on the Internet.

What is the one indisputable fact about computers connected to the internet? Answer: they are totally insecure. We should surely have learned by this time that when we enter private or secret information of any kind we might just as well broadcast it over the radio or post it on the front page of *The New York Times*. Trusting the entire electoral process to the Internet is not just asking for trouble, it is begging for trouble.

Those of us who were born before 1960 remember, assuming we remember anything, how we used to vote in the ancient days before computers. I seem to recall voting on a piece on paper by placing one or several crosses on it. Most of us could make crosses on paper, it was simple and democratic, and no machines were required. These crosses were then added and counted by ordinary human beings, citizens, in secure conditions and held, also under heavy guard, until a result was announced. Citizens did the counting, not a computer that might or might not be connected to Moscow or Beijing, or even Tehran or Kabul. I must have voted dozens of times like this and I never remember seeing KGB officers lurking in the corners of the local polling station.

Then came the mechanical voting machines, designed to simplify voting for those not talented enough to make a cross on a piece of paper. I never trusted those machines where you pulled a lever down to vote, they seemed too much like casino slots, and were probably rigged in the same way. Then, after the manual voting machines, came the computers.

The computers are the problem. In saying this I know that I have committed the twenty-first century version of sacrilege. But really, hasn't anyone noticed that this marvelous gift of computing power has an absolutely poisonous side to it? Everything is connected, including voting machines, campaign offices, and the whole bureaucracy of the election. *Wired* magazine describes the entire setup as "Absurdly vulnerable," and they ought to know. So dump the wretched electronic voting machines into a large pit in the Arizona desert. They're probably made in China anyway, and getting rid of them will be a bonanza for the paper and printing industries. We can start again with paper ballots and all-human counting. It may be tedious and slow, but at least the results won't be tabulated in the Kremlin.

Some states, including Connecticut, continue to use paper ballots counted by hand in national elections. In these states there is no possibility of direct interference with voting via the Internet, so there's nothing to worry about. However eighteen states have been named as having highly vulnerable voting systems, including Delaware, Georgia, Louisiana, New Jersey and South Carolina.

The paper ballot counted by hand isn't a perfect system. Election tampering goes back more than two thousand years to the days of ancient Rome, and I'm not suggesting that the *results* would be any better, only that they would be the real results. We voters are not particularly smart. As Winston Churchill remarked: "The best argument against democracy is a five-minute conversation with the average voter" and, if we insist on voting for useless politicians we are going to get useless politicians, so our situation will be no better than before. But at least, if we have a secure electoral system, we will be able to say with confidence that it is entirely our own fault.

In the Footsteps of Zeus

"I am not fit for this office and should never have been here."
President Warren G. Harding

We spend more time arguing and worrying about the unknown Presidents of the future than about the semi-mythical Presidents of the past. Yet the past is full of lessons, messages, hints and metaphors that still give food for thought, if only we pause to think.

The role of modern Presidents is not unlike that of the gods of ancient Greece and Rome. The gods represented certain important ideas or principles, and they had the power to set events in motion but not to control them. They were insulated from the ordinary population by layers of lesser gods. At its most imperial the role of the President corresponds to that of Jupiter or Zeus the chief god of the ancient world, whose symbol was the eagle and who was very fond of casting thunderbolts and otherwise throwing his weight around. The men who framed the Constitution were educated in the classics, which is why Washington DC looks and functions so eerily like ancient Rome. The founders knew all about the Olympians, and they never quite abandoned the imperial idea even as they created a democratic constitution. In December 2020 Donald

Trump, in the last days of his Presidency, issued an executive order that all new government buildings in Washington should be in the classical (i.e. Roman Imperial) style, rather than modern designs. His meaning and his fantasy could scarcely be clearer.

All Presidents inherit the uneasy compromise of 1787. They are expected to be amiable and Olympian, democratic and commanding, all at the same time. It's impossible. Real life Presidents tend to wobble from one extreme to the other. Alexis de Tocqueville, the French aristocrat who came to America in 1835, was one of the first to write about this uneasy balancing act. He was convinced that democracy was better than monarchy, but worried that democracy would produce nothing but mediocre and capricious leaders because most voters would mistrust candidates with superior talent or intelligence. H. L. Mencken took the argument a step further in the 1920s when he argued that if we keep voting for presidents who seem just like us we will end up with a President who *is* just like us, just a regular imperfect human being, instead of the extraordinarily gifted and talented individual we really need. Something like this happened in 2016, and perhaps in 2020.

Washington and Lincoln loom large in history because they were extraordinary men, and not regular, likeable guys. They had the gift of leadership, a word much spoken today but rarely put into practice. Leadership meant getting out in front, even at the risk of unpopularity. Both Washington and Lincoln attracted their share of hatred and abuse in their own lifetimes. Modern politicians can't afford the luxury of getting out in front. They can't afford to be visionaries. They must converge towards the ambiguous center, trying to embrace every contradictory viewpoint to please the maximum number of voters while at the same time expressing complete certainty about everything. Modern Presidents and Presidential candidates don't share their doubts in public, as Lincoln and Washington often did. They act as if everything is under control. It's the grand illusion, the shadow of leadership without the substance.

Vox populi, vox dei, as the Romans might have said before the Emperors came along and changed the rules: the voice of the people is the voice of god. Today, Washington and Lincoln would never get past the first primary. If we stay with the metaphor of ancient Rome it might be safer if not wiser put gung-ho leaders like Jupiter into retirement and choose from among the lesser slate of deities. A likely candidate from the Roman Parthenon would seem to be Minerva Goddess of Wisdom running as an Independent of course. But then Minerva, following the time-honored practice of trying to appeal to everybody was, in her spare time, also the goddess of war and warriors. Even the gods are not perfect.

The Problem of "Leadership"

"You are free, and that is why you are lost."
Franz Kafka

Truth is always the first casualty in an election, as in a war. In the electoral process the English language suffers some nasty injuries. Consider, among many examples, the idea of "leadership." The word has been trumpeted around and fought over as if it was a universally accepted virtue, like wisdom or honesty. But leadership is just a neutral quality, like energy. It is not good or bad in itself. Leadership can take you to the top of the mountain or push you over a cliff. There's nothing more depressing than hearing intelligent people crying out for leadership. Someone will be only too happy to provide it.

If we look to history, as we always should, we can certainly find great leaders, like Franklin D. Roosevelt, Dr. Martin Luther King, and Winston Churchill. But if we consider political leadership down the ages it seems obvious that, on the whole, the suffering citizens of the world would have been better off without it. Think of some of the most famous political leaders of the past two thousand years: Genghis Khan, Julius Caesar, Alexander, Napoleon, Hitler,

Lenin, Stalin, and Mao. Powerful leaders may be exciting to read about, but their legacy tends to be an enormous body count, and one or several destroyed societies.

Historically, strong leadership has usually been a problem rather than a solution, because strong leadership depends on weak citizenship. The leader's job is to convince the rest of us that he or she knows best. This is absolutely never the case, as recent history has so vividly demonstrated. The role of the followers (the citizens, that's us) is to do what we are told, and not to think too hard about it, or take any responsibility for it. That's not democracy, that's sheep herding. The British Prime Minister Disraeli got it the right way around when he quipped: "I must follow the people. Am I not their leader?"

It is so easy and tempting to fall for the leadership ploy. Reasoned argument and democratic debate are slow and difficult. Leadership is swift and simple, and very often violent because that's the easy way to get people's attention. The civil rights campaigner Ralph Bunche said: "There are no warlike peoples—only warlike leaders."

The social media have put leadership on steroids. This began with Hitler's effective use of radio in the 1930s, and now a leader can lie to millions of people directly. Ambitious leaders can construct a kind of parallel universe of lies and conspiracies to justify their power—it has happened over and over again in history. Social media also allow mobs to be conjured very quickly out of thin air—the so-called "flash mob"—like a phantom army always ready to obey the leader's whim. If that's not dangerous I don't know what is.

So, where do we go from here? There were always lies, and there were always mobs, including the one that started the French Revolution. What these kinds of events have always had in common is what George Washington called "the spirit of faction," the apparently irresistible urge to encourage division and tribalism.

Perhaps we simply need a break—a political season without wild ideological rhetoric and silly games, with a government devoted to administration, statesmanship abroad, and problem-solving at home. This would give politicians time to think, and something to think about. Meanwhile the rest of us would have four years without leadership, which may be exactly the kind of leadership we need.

Rough Justice

"The most effective way to destroy people is to deny and obliterate their own understanding of their history."
George Orwell

"If we consider the shortness of human life, and our limited knowledge even of what passes in our own time, we must be sensible that we would be forever children in understanding were it not for our knowledge of history."
David Hume

When Abraham Lincoln addressed the United States Congress in 1863, he began with these words: "Fellow citizens, we cannot escape history."

It was a wonderful, a noble sentiment, and perhaps it was true then. But it's not true now. Not only *can* we escape history, we *have* escaped history, by the simple process of forgetting it.

The schools have done their part to promote this historical amnesia. The Department of Education reported that six out of ten high school seniors couldn't say how the United States came into existence. (The answer is: through illegal rebellion against the legitimate authority of the British King). Fifty per cent of high school seniors couldn't say what the Cold War was. (The answer is: the

Cold War was a political mistake, but an economic stroke of genius). National history knowledge tests show that most fourth-graders can't identify the opening passage of the Declaration of Independence, and that most high school seniors can't explain the checks-and-balances theory that is (or in pre-Trump days used to be) the rationale behind the three branches of the United States government. These young people will be voting soon.

A Senate panel considered legislation that would expand national testing on the subject of US history, and a pilot program was set up to do just that. But there's no point in testing, and then throwing up our hands in horror at the results, and then doing nothing about it. Part of the problem is that it's hard to teach real history today. It's too full of dynamite political correctness issues that can blow a teacher right out of a job. It's too carved up into tiny fiefdoms: black history, women's history, gay history, and so on. It is impossible to make any sense of American history as a whole.

Anyone who tries to teach non-ideological history is also up against the mass media, and especially movies, television, and video games, which present a bizarre version of the past that consists entirely of conflicts and battles in the Hollywood style between good guys and bad guys. No wonder the kids do badly on their tests. All they know about the past is that was nasty, and that it is gone. People in history have the bad taste to be dead, which certainly won't happen to us. They were unsophisticated, wore funny clothes, and listened to un-amplified non-digitalized music in the days when the only way you could get surround sound was to have several musicians sitting in different positions in a room. Who needs to know about *them?*

This is obviously something to be considered by Presidents who worry about their historical legacy. They also need to consider that administrations that do nothing to improve the dreadful state of history education will be forgotten whatever they do. That's rough, but it is justice.

The Survival of the Fittest

> "We live in a system that espouses merit, equality, and a level playing field, but exalts those with wealth, power, and celebrity, however gained."
> **Derrick A. Bell**

In my family everyone was assumed to be honest and trustworthy unless they showed some obvious contrary evidence, such as a prison uniform or a knife dripping with blood. It's hard to hold on to this benign view of humanity today. Now, like Hercule Poirot, we must suspect everyone of everything.

Our faith in human nature has taken a beating right across the board, from the bottom to all the way to the top. For most of our lives my now-elderly generation had assumed that scientific research must be serious and honest, and that bankers were sober and trustworthy people. We believed implicitly that school grades, athletic performances, prescription medications and company accounts were more or less what they appeared to be. Not anymore. Our trust in our fellow man (and woman) has been worn down and worn out by millions of advertisements and campaign ads that are indistinguishable from lies, decades of telephone scams of every conceivable kind, and by a deluge of trickery and criminality on the Internet. We are the daily target of credit card scams, time-share scams, tax scams, identity theft scams: if you can imagine a dishonest trick you can be sure that somebody else thought of it already, and has probably tied it on you. We read every day about teachers who fix grades all the way up to bankers who fix entire markets, politicians who fix elections, researchers who fix results, doctors who fix Medicare payments, and criminal religious leaders. Air force officers have been cheating on their tests, and the King of Spain's daughter was charged with money laundering. Everybody wants to get in on the game. Even the fake news can scarcely be believed, and most conspiracy theories are frankly incredible. There are disturbing rumors that even our most exalted political leaders sometimes fail to speak the exact truth. Only Pollyanna herself could fail to get the message: lies work, lies win.

Of course we want to live in a society open to talent. Study and hard work can achieve anything, and all the old barriers to success like family background, race and gender have been swept away by the irresistible movement towards equal opportunity. We can't be suspicious of everything and everybody all the time. It's not fair, and it's not true in most cases. But we have to be careful. How can we believe the padded résumés, the certificates on the wall, the stock prospectus, the tempting invitations on the internet, or the nightly news? If a profession or business tells us: "We're on your side, we care, you can trust us" we mistrust them at once.

A sociology professor called Michael Young predicted all this sixty years ago, in a book called *The Rise of the Meritocracy*. Many readers were blindsided by the word "meritocracy." It had a fine ring to it, suggesting to my naïve young mind that the best, most capable and most trustworthy people would rise to the top—a true hierarchy of merit. The future belonged to people with superior qualities of character, knowledge, and honesty, people we could trust. Nobody could argue with that.

I still have my copy of the first edition of *The Rise of the Meritocracy*. It is in brand new condition, which shows that I didn't read it properly. If I had paid attention, I would have seen that Professor Young's vision of the future was more depressing than inspiring. He offered a pessimistic fantasy of a world in which the cunning strategy of the elite was to *really give* equal opportunity to everyone, in a kind of libertarian free-for-all, no holds barred. Honesty had nothing to do with it. The most manipulative and ruthless people of every race and class and both sexes fought their way to the top, and all those left behind (the vast majority, the less competitive ninety-nine percent) were left without any power or voice. This was a meritocracy without empathy, a self-perpetuating elite of manipulators, technocrats, power brokers, and money managers. There was nothing noble or superior about them. It was Social Darwinism in its purest form—the survival of the fittest.

What the survival of the fittest guarantees is that those who rise to the top are precisely the ones we would least want to have at the top. But it's useless to complain, we are up against a law of nature here. Who or whatever can do best in a particular environment will succeed. A penguin won't survive long in the Sahara Desert, or an unwary mouse in a house full of cats. Ancient civilizations favored warriors who were brave and loyal. We have created an environment that favors tricksters and cheats. We have evolved from a meritocracy based on courage to one based on cunning.

So we have to face the fact that our present elites and leaders must be the best adapted to this society as it now exists. It's a chilling thought because that makes the rest of us feel like flightless penguins at the equator. If the heat doesn't get us the predators will.

Michael Young's book had only one answer to this: to create a revolution which, in the story, inevitably fails because that's the way the survival of the fittest works. Fortunately, the tale is nothing but a clever and cynical piece of fiction.

Note: Two books were publishd on this very subject in 2020:

Head, Hand, Heart by David Goodhart suggests that the elevation of graduation and graduates has led to a devaluation of skills (hands) and hearts (caring professions)

The Tyranny of Merit: What's become of the common good? By Michael J. Sandel argues that the US is being torn apart by the artificial separation of degree holders (one thid of population) and the rest, creating a kind of "tyranny of merit" with no concern for the common good.

Do You Believe in Magic?

*"The consolation of imaginary things is
not an imaginary consolation."*
Roger Scruton

It was a stroke of genius by the framers of the Constitution to schedule the elections immediately after Halloween. We are in the right frame of mind- so thoroughly accustomed to thin disguises, thinly-disguised blackmail, and magical thinking that we can no longer tell the difference between fact and fantasy.

Halloween is not an easy time for those of us brought up to respect the principles of the Enlightenment. According to those principles, we human beings can only take our next step forward by banishing all our fantastic supernatural beliefs, and building a world based on scientific knowledge and humanistic principles. On Halloween we take several steps backwards. In the eighteenth century, philosophers like Voltaire confidently expected that superstition—"That infamous thing" as he called it—would soon vanish, and that the world would move into a golden age of reason and science. How disappointed he would be to see us now, still captivated by some of the oldest and silliest superstitions and magical beliefs.

We have science, yes, but we seem to want magic too. So if the philosopher Voltaire, arrived in Long Island in

October he would find us surrounded by monsters, ghosts and dancing skeletons, preparing for All Hallow's Eve, the eve of witches. He would find alive and well many of the magical and superstitious beliefs he sneered at on his deathbed in 1778: He would be astonished to discover people in the twenty-first century wearing lucky charms and copper bracelets, playing with Tarot cards, insisting that bad news comes in threes, buying lottery tickets, and chasing after instant cures for all diseases. He would see us watching Superman movies (pure medieval magic stuff), crying every year over the Wizard of Oz, and playing sword and sorcery video games. He could go to a bookstore, if he could find one, and look at the New Age section (a label Voltaire would surely have found hilariously funny), and find shelves of books about astrology, reincarnation, mysterious earth forces, magic crystals, flying saucers and every kind of superstitious twaddle handed down to us from the dark ages, when magic ruled. They weren't called the dark ages for nothing. Necromancers claimed to raise the spirits of the dead and put them into communication with the living, just as spiritualistic mediums do nowadays. And alchemy, perhaps the most highly-organized form of magic, offered the alluring prospect of unlimited gold out of dross—exactly like a modern-day investment analyst, and with similar results.

Voltaire understood all too well that there are no hidden forces, although there may be secret ones. The Caped Avenger won't save us, but on the other hand, the Galactic Evil Empire is unlikely to blow up the universe. What we see around us is what we get—the ordinary human muddle, full of uncertainty, and ambiguity. "Doubt is not a pleasant condition," wrote Voltaire, "But certainty is absurd."

The desire to believe in magic seems almost to be hard wired. All our myths and stories show it. The magical universe, as imagined by Hollywood, is invariably divided into good guys and bad guys, both endowed with supernatural powers. Every Force must have a Dark Side. Every Harry Potter must have a Lord Voldemort; Batman has the Joker; Frodo Baggins has Lord Sauron (why so many evil lords, I wonder?); Superman has Lex Luthor; and the good witch of the north must contend with a wicked witch of the east. It has even been slyly suggested by some European critics that, due to an unfortunate confusion between Hollywood story lines and real life, magical myths of good and evil provide the basis for a lot of our politics and foreign policies.

The problem with magic is that it doesn't work, and the problem with human beings was and is that they want to believe in it anyway. Magic is easy and quick. Science is slow, and difficult, and it doesn't even pretend to answer our most urgent metaphysical questions. Why bother with the ambiguities of science when magical thinking can solve everything, with no mental effort whatsoever?

I suspect that magic stays in our minds as a kind of primitive, hopeful faith, and even a rebellion against the hardness of facts. Plenty of people take advantage of our half-conscious belief in it, including legions of advertisers and politicians. Magic promises a short cut through all the complexities and disappointments of life, directly to our hearts desire. It's hard resist believing in magic just a little, even though it always turns out to be a trick rather than a treat.

Vote with Your Head

Presidential elections are emotional events, and that's bad. Elections are supposed to be based on thoughtful policies and sensible choices. Modern democracy was an invention of the Age of Reason, the eighteenth century. But today's elections seem more like an invitation to indulge our most *un*reasonable feelings.

Feelings are fine, within reason, but they should be reserved for situations where nothing important is at stake, like sports or TV reality shows. Then everyone can scream and shout and emote to their heart's content, no damage done. But, at election time. we need to lock the emotions in the closet and *think*.

Thinking takes time, which no politician has these days. Their advisers and campaign managers must think for them. But they have no time either. Campaigns moves at a manic pace, reactions must be instant, reflection is utterly impossible. The result is like one of those Roadrunner cartoons where Wiley E. Coyote pursues the Roadrunner in an eternal battle of need versus speed, aggravation versus acceleration. They never stop to discuss things.

It all makes good TV and is entertaining for the voters. But it is no way to decide who should preside over the government of the most powerful country in the world.

We usually have a binary choice between candidates and programs that are relatively emotional on one hand and relatively rational on the other, although nothing is ever quite so clear cut. Religion and patriotism, fear and resentment, race and class are all tossed into the mix to make the choice less easy, and to activate those dangerous emotions. Add in irrational loyalties, such as "My party right or wrong," as if this was a sports event, and the trite slogans and childish conspiracy theories whipped up by the social media, and you have the perfect prescription for an election choice that is about a thoughtful as a five-year old choosing ice cream with sprinkles over ice cream without. Even George Orwell never imagined that populations would voluntarily embrace what he called doublethink—the willingness to embrace two or more contradictory ideas at once.

It wouldn't be a bad idea to have a National "Let's Stop and Think About This Day" just before each election, with all the chattering voices silenced, the ingratiating faces off the screens, and each voter engaged in considering the facts and making the most rational choice possible. But that's not going to happen. It would ruin the game.

In any case we can't think clearly if we don't know what the facts are, and what politicians tell us is scripted by doublespeak professionals who have made this empty Orwellian language into an art form. This leaves a great many things hidden, including the real beliefs and motivations of politicians themselves—in other words, the plain truth. I know the plain truth has never been tried in the whole history of politics, but there has to be a first time.

Since we can't make much sense of what candidates say, it all comes down to how they look, and how we feel about them. This may be a good way to choose a piece of fish or a new hat, but it's an insane way to choose a political leader. We need to know what *they* know, what they *think, if* they think, and what they would say to us, if only they could find the words.

It's All About the Money

"We have now sunk to a depth at which the restatement of the obvious is the first duty of intelligent men."
George Orwell

When citizens vote in congressional and presidential elections they often fail to ask themselves: why would any sane person want to be in politics right now? The imaginary "debates" about imaginary "policies" only confuse the issue, as they are intended to do. Ideology has nothing to do with it. It's all about the money.

Politics is a job like any other, but more rewarding than most. We are voting the winners into an incredibly desirable jobs, offering prestige, a whole lot of money, lifelong security, excellent health care—and virtually no responsibility. Congressmen have almost no independent power, any more that airline pilots. They go where the control tower sends them, and they always end up where they started, but they are very well paid for it. We can't vote for a program because the parties are infinitely flexible in their beliefs. What matters is to get into power, and if possible stay in and support your team. But that's not what we hear. Are they going to mention this when they ask for our vote? No.

Elections are about illusions and handouts, power, and enormous amounts of money—not only the obscene cost of the campaigns but the enormous amount that individual Congressional candidates hope to gain: $174,000 *for life* for house and senate members and the ability to vote themselves pay raises plus unbeatable health care and lifetime pensions, plus expenses and a helping hand with pocket money from the hundreds of lobbying organizations in Washington. These are pretty rich rewards for sitting in a Congress that scarcely accomplishes anything for years at a time.

As political campaigns move entirely to TV and the social media, the only essential thing will be money. This will simplify the democratic process. The biggest fundraisers will buy the most and best commercials and will win automatically. In fact, in a rational future, we might just get rid of the whole tiresome electoral process, and simply hand the country over to the candidates who have pocketed the most money by election date. In American terms they are by definition winners, and deserve to be richly rewarded.

This is the only job with such rich rewards that is open to anyone, even those without the qualifications, character of intelligence to compete in the outside world. Even a criminal record or mental derangement are not necessarily a barrier to political success. *"There is no distinctively American criminal class except Congress"* wrote Mark Twain. Only those who enter the lottery have a chance of winning the big prize. So why not grab a ticket?

The Only Thing That Might Work

Anyone who voted in 2020 must have been impressed as I was by the sheer number of people who turned out, sometimes standing in the rain for hours. I'm not speaking about the result (which was ambiguous) or about the process (which was crazy), but the *participation*, especially when so many people had so much else to worry about. Sixty-five percent voted, up from less than half in recent elections. This is not bad, considering how much of the population is completely disgusted with politics and would not vote for anyone under any circumstances. Enough people cared about this one, enough to give up their time and their comfort and take the risk of infection. That's pretty impressive, and that's what democracy is supposed to be like, but rarely is.

The ancient Greeks and Romans created a limited kind of democracy more than two thousand years ago. It was far from perfect. Voters suffered from pressure, propaganda, intimidation and bribery, but at least there were no social media. Roman citizens voted by areas or tribes, much like us. Thousands had to stand in line to vote publicly and individually, sun or rain. Sometimes it took all day. The Romans kept their fragile democracy for five hundred years, much longer than we have so far, but it was never popular with the rich and powerful. When the Emperors came along they simply swept the elections aside, and that was the end of the Roman experiment with democracy.

Of course we are nothing like ancient Rome, apart from the imperial architecture in Washington DC, the wealthy and powerful senate, and the hugely expensive military machine. Those are just accidental similarities. But even our modern democracy is a fragile thing, too easily flipped into autocracy, as it was in Rome, by ruthless people with an unlimited greed for money and power. Being a developed first-world country has nothing to do with it. Europe has provided some sobering examples recently.

Democracy is at its most vulnerable when there are two sides divided more or less fifty-fifty, who cannot engage in rational discussion. Whatever happens half the population will be elated and half will be angry—not a good recipe for national unity, or any sort of progress.

This seems to be empathetically the case after the 2020 election. We have at least two nations here, and this is nothing new. There were two nations when Lincoln was elected in 1840, and they eventually chose to fight. This carries on a venerable European tradition, going back a thousand years, in which meaningless divisions caused perpetual and equally meaningless conflict. Guy Fawkes was a Catholic plotting to blow up the Protestant British parliament in 1605, but it could just as well have been the other way around. These divisions provided the excuse for continuous wars, which men enjoy so much. The idiocy of the doctrines never seemed to discourage anyone from dying for them. If religion was not enough, people were always eager to fight over issues of heredity, territory and, of course, money.

Sometimes the goals of a rebellion are specific and achievable. But the violently angry groups of the twenty-first century—a substantial fraction of the population—seem to be gripped by a furious desire for something unachievable, something they can barely even name. They want an authoritarian leader who will leave them completely free, prosperity without the discipline of work, Christianity without the New Testament, women back 'in their place,' and white supremacy without any justification other than skin color. They also want guns, pickup trucks, and unlimited government handouts without taxes. It is not a very practical program, but it makes a lot of people feel empowered.

While we are counting up discontented groups we mustn't forget radical feminists, religious fanatics, African Americans, revolutionary socialists, and radical ecologists, all pulling in different directions. All these rebels are irreconcilable and unappeasable, like angry children. Nothing could make them happy except a fantasy turned into reality—a nation all of their own.

The great project of the twentieth century was nation building. Countries like Germany and Italy were created from a mass of fragmented states and principalities, and the "United States" seemed to become one huge nation under one government and one constitution. This was achieved by enormous brutality—essentially genocide—in the west, and by civil war against the south. The cracks in this uneasy federation are now all too obvious. America is clearly two nations, or perhaps three or four.

In this unhappy situation, one President is clearly not enough to satisfy everybody. We need, at the very least, two Presidents. There are historical precedents. The Roman Emperor Diocletian devised a system of two emperors, called Augustus and Caesar respectively. And from 1378 to 1417 there were two Popes, one in Avignon and one in Rome. Napoleon, to placate his useless and demanding relatives, created little kingdoms for them to rule over, so they could do as they liked and imagine themselves free. That's my modest proposal: two Presidents, representing two different populations and promoting two different sets of policies. Like he two popes they could spend their time abusing and denouncing one another. Everyone would be happy, knowing that *their* chosen President was in his own personal White House. Nothing would get done, of course, but nothing gets done now.

A little shifting of populations would be necessary, so that everyone could feel comfortable and safe with their right-thinking neighbors. We could start with the good old Mason Dixon line, with one President ruling from the middle of a golf course in Florida, and the other perhaps from a small town in Vermont. Of course, two nations might not be nearly enough. Peculiar states like Texas, Utah and California could become independent nations and follow their peculiarities all the way. The great heartland would continue to be a problem for government, and might have to be abandoned to its own retrograde version of nationhood, a sort of latter-day anarchic macho cowboy utopia. In fact there is almost no limit to this process of devolution. Since the 1990s Ethiopia has had nine ethnically-based states, each with its own leader and the right to secede. The process of national fragmentation has been going on all around the world. Every religious, ideological and ethnic group wants its own nation, and perhaps the great global project of the twenty-first century will be to give every group of discontented citizens a place where they could be happy, their own ideal territory like a big gated community, shared only by people exactly like them in every way.

It sounds fantastic, and even ridiculous. Most brilliant ideas do at first. But it's the only thing that might work.

www.ingramcontent.com/pod-product-compliance
Lightning Source LLC
LaVergne TN
LVHW021652060526
838200LV00050B/2320